Stand Out 2

Grammar Challenge

Second Edition

HEINLE
CENGAGE Learning

Australia • Brazil • Japan • Korea • Mexico • Singapore • Spain • United Kingdom • United States

HEINLE
CENGAGE Learning

Stand Out 2 Grammar Challenge
Rob Jenkins and Staci Johnson

Publisher: Sherrise Roehr

Acquisitions Editor: Tom Jefferies

Director of Content and Media Production:
Michael Burggren

Development Editor: Michael Ryall

Product Marketing Manager: Katie Kelley

Sr. Content Project Editor: Maryellen E. Killeen

Sr. Print Buyer: Mary Beth Hennebury

Development Editor: Carol Crowell

Project Manager: Tunde A. Dewey

Cover / Text Designer: Studio Montage

Compositor: Parkwood Composition
Service, Inc.

ISBN 10: 1-4240-0991-X
ISBN 13: 978-1-4240-0991-6

Heinle
25 Thomson Place
Boston, MA 02210
USA

Cengage Learning is a leading provider of customized learning solutions with office locations around the globe, including Singapore, the United Kingdom, Australia, Mexico, Brazil and Japan. Locate our local office at:
international.cengage.com/region

Cengage Learning products are represented in Canada
by Nelson Education, Ltd.

Visit Heinle online at **elt.heinle.com**
Visit our corporate website at **cengage.com**

Printed in the United States of America
5 6 7 8 9 10   15 14 13 12 11

CONTENTS

TO THE TEACHER

Stand Out 2 Grammar Challenge challenges students to develop and expand their grammar skills through fifty-nine guided exercises or "challenges."

Each Challenge includes:

▶ **Charts** Clear grammar charts help the teacher lay out the components of structures and provide useful example sentences.

▶ **Notes** Notes within the charts help students understand important shifts in language use and meaning through concise explanations.

▶ **Practice** Exercises challenge students to master grammar structures while reviewing the vocabulary and thematic contexts actively taught in *Stand Out 2 Student Book*. Additional exercises reinforce grammar structures passively introduced in *Stand Out 2 Student Book* contexts.

How to use the *Stand Out 2 Grammar Challenge* workbook

The *Stand Out 2 Grammar Challenge* workbook can be used in a variety of ways:

• The grammar challenges can be assigned daily or on an as-needed basis.

• The grammar challenges can be completed individually, with a partner, or as a class.

• Students may complete challenges at home or in the classroom.

• Instructors can provide guided feedback upon completion, or ask students to self-correct or peer-edit. All exercises are formatted to provide for ease of correction and assessment.

• The *Grammar Challenge 2* answer key is available to teachers on the *Stand Out* website at: **standout.heinle.com**. It can be printed out for student use.

• The grammar challenges need not be followed in any particular order within a unit. Some challenges will be review for students, while others will reinforce the newer structures from *Stand Out 2 Student Book*.

• The *Stand Out 2 Grammar Challenge* workbook is an effective supplement in a multi-level classroom because it challenges the highly motivated students while providing support for students who need extra reinforcement.

The appendix includes a glossary of grammar terms with examples. This is intended as a reference for both students and teachers, but it is not intended that all these terms will be understood at this level. The appendix also includes grammar charts from the *Stand Out 2 Grammar Challenge* workbook as well as lists of irregular verbs and verb conjugations.

However you choose to use it, you'll find that the *Stand Out 2 Grammar Challenge* workbook is a flexible and effective grammar tool for teachers and students seeking challenging grammar instruction.

Simple Present: Be *(sidebar)*

Welcome to Our Class

CHALLENGE 1 ➤ Simple Present: *Be*

A Look at the information.

Mario   Katrina   Alexi   Lien

fine   tired   hungry   angry

B Read the conversation.

Mario: Hi, Katrina. How are you?
Katrina: Hello, Mario. I'm tired. I need some rest. How are you?
Mario: I'm fine. Thanks.

C Write a conversation with Alexi and Lien. Then, practice with a friend.

Alexi: _____

Lien: _____

Alexi: _____

D Read the chart.

Simple Present: *Be* (Contractions)			
Subject	***Be* Verb**	**Feelings**	**Example sentence**
I	am	fine nervous	I **am** fine. (I**'m** fine.)
you, we, they	are	sad tired happy	You **are** tired. (You**'re** tired.) We **are** hungry. (We**'re** hungry.) They **are** nervous. (They**'re** nervous.)
he, she, it	is	angry hungry	He **is** happy. (He**'s** happy.) She **is** angry. (She**'s** angry.)

E Talk to others in class using words from the "Feelings" and "*Be* verb" columns from the chart in Exercise D.

F Complete the sentences with the correct form of *be*.

Contractions

1. I ___am___ tired. I need some rest.
2. Maria and Paul _____ hungry.
3. We _____ fine. How are you?
4. He _____ angry. He needs our help.
5. The children _____ nervous. It's exam day.
6. She _____ happy. She has good friends.
7. You _____ sad. Can I help you?
8. The dog _____ hungry. Feed it, please.

1. ___I'm___ tired.
2. _____ hungry.
3. _____ fine.
4. _____ angry.
5. _____ nervous.
6. _____ happy.
7. _____ sad.
8. _____ hungry.

G Match sentences with feelings. Draw a line.

1. She needs some rest.
2. They have a test today.
3. We have a new baby!
4. He wants a hamburger.
5. I have no friends.

a. sad
b. hungry
c. nervous
d. tired
e. happy

H Write sentences with the information from Exercise G.

1. She's tired. She needs some rest.
2. _____
3. _____
4. _____
5. _____

I Write two feelings you have on a piece of paper. Then, talk to five students. Write the information in the chart below.

Name	Feeling	Feeling
John	tired	hungry
1.		
2.		
3.		
4.		
5.		

Welcome to Our Class

CHALLENGE 2 ➤ Possessive Adjectives

A Read the registration form.

Evans Adult School Registration Form

PERSONAL INFORMATION

Name: _____   Phone: ( )
           Last   First

Birth Date: _____

Street Address: _____

City: _____   State: _____   Zip Code: _____

B Write the information in the form above.

Jonathan Smith	(714)	January 14, 2010
555-8989	March 3, 1978	Pine City
California	2356 Orchard Lane	90638

C Read the chart.

Possessive Adjectives		
Pronoun	**Possessive adjective**	**Example sentence**
I	my	**My** address is 3356 Archer Blvd.
you	your	**Your** phone number is 555-5678.
he	his	**His** last name is Jones.
she	her	**Her** first name is Lien.
it	its	**Its** name is Crystal River Dam.
we	our	**Our** teacher is Mr. Kelley.
they	their	**Their** home is in Sausalito.

Complete the sentences with possessive adjectives.

1. I live in a big house. _____My_____ house is on Orchard Lane.

2. Please call Maria and Jonathan. _____ phone number is 555-8989.

3. You have a new zip code. _____ zip code is 90638.

4. We need a delivery, please. _____ address is 2356 Orchard Lane.

5. He lives in a big city. _____ city is next to Riverton.

6. Maria's husband is young. _____ birth date is March 3, 1978.

7. The motel is famous. _____ name is Dew Drop Inn.

 Using the information in the chart, complete the sentences below.

(Kenji Nakamura)

Lincoln Adult School
2274 W. Bayside Drive
San Francisco, CA
August 12, 1985

(Marie Alexander)

Lincoln Adult School
32 W. Palm Dr.
San Francisco, CA
June 5, 1975

1. Kenji lives in an apartment. _____ address is _____.

2. Marie and Kenji go to school. _____ school is _____.

3. Marie is older than Kenji. _____ birth date is _____.

4. Marie and Kenji live in the same state. _____ state is _____.

5. Kenji is from Japan. _____ last name is _____.

6. We live in San Francisco with _____ friend, Kenji.

F **Talk to a classmate and complete the chart. Tell a group.**

My address is _____ _____	My classmate's address is _____ _____
My hobbies are _____ _____	His/her hobbies are _____ _____
My school is _____ _____	Our teacher is _____ _____

Possessive Adjectives

Questions with Can

Welcome to Our Class

CHALLENGE 3 ➤ Questions with *Can*

A Read the paragraph.

Teacher and Student

    A teacher needs to talk to many students at the same time. It is important that students participate. They need the practice. Ask for help when you don't understand. Speak in English for practice. Talk to the teacher, and he or she will help you. You can say, *"I don't understand."* You can also ask the teacher or students questions. For example, one question could be, *"Can you say that again?"*

B Read the sentences and questions.

Please speak slower.	I'm sorry. I don't understand.	Excuse me?
Please speak louder.	Can you say that again, please?	Can you spell that?

C What sentences and questions do you say more? Rank them 1-6 in order of how often you use them. Number 1 is the most often and 6 is the least often used.

_____ I'm sorry. I don't understand.

_____ Please speak slower.

_____ Please speak louder.

_____ Excuse me?

_____ Can you say that again, please?

_____ Can you spell that?

D Read the chart.

Questions with *Can*			
Question word	**Subject**	**Verb**	**Example sentence**
can	you	help	**Can** you help me?
		answer	**Can** you answer the question?
		repeat	**Can** you repeat it again, please?
		say	**Can** you say it again, please?
		speak	**Can** you speak slower?
		spell	**Can** you spell that, please?

P6   Pre-Unit

E Use the words to write questions.

1. you / spell that / can   _____ Can you spell that? _____

2. say that again / can / you   _____

3. that / you / can / repeat   _____

4. speak louder / you / can   _____

5. can / you / help me   _____

6. you / slower / can / speak   _____

7. English / you / teach me / can   _____

8. open the door / can / you   _____

9. write it / you / can   _____

F Match the problems with the questions.

1. The teacher speaks very fast.
2. The room is hot.
3. You didn't hear it all.
4. You don't know how to write it.
5. You need to talk to the teacher.

a. Can I talk to you after class?
b. Can you repeat that?
c. Can you speak slower?
d. Can you spell that, please?
e. Can you turn on the air-conditioning?

G Read the conversation below and write a new one with a partner. Use ideas from Exercise F.

Student A: I have a problem. Can you help me?

Student B: Sure.

Student A: You speak very fast. Can you speak slower in class?

Student B: OK.

Student A: _____

Student B: _____

Student A: _____

Student B: _____

Everyday Life

CHALLENGE 1 ➤ Simple Present: *Live* and *Be*

 Read about the students.

Kenji	Anya	Gilberto	Marie
single	married	single	divorced
22 years old	68 years old	30 years old	32 years old
Los Angeles	Los Angeles	Los Angeles	Los Angeles

 Complete the chart.

Name	Marital status	Age	Residence
Kenji	single		
Anya			
Gilberto			
Marie			

C **Read the charts.**

Simple Present: *Live*			
Subject	Verb	Residence	Example sentence
I, we, you, they	live	in Los Angeles in California	I **live** in Los Angeles. You **live** in Los Angeles, California.
he, she	lives	in the United States in Mexico	He **lives** in the United States. She **lives** in Mexico.

Simple Present: *Be*			
Subject	Verb	Residence	Example sentence
I	am	from Mexico	I **am** from Mexico. *(I'm)*
we, you, they	are	single 23 years old	We **are** single. *(We're)* You **are** 23 years old. *(You're)*
he, she	is	divorced from Vietnam	He **is** divorced. *(He's)* She **is** from Vietnam. *(She's)*

D Complete the sentences with the correct form of *live* or *be*.

1. He _____lives_____ in Tallahassee, Florida.

2. We _____ from Michigan.

3. They _____ divorced.

4. The students _____ from China.

5. I _____ 50 years old.

6. Jennifer _____ in Santa Barbara.

7. You _____ in a house on Washington St.

8. We _____ in the United States.

9. Jacob _____ 18 years old.

10. My teacher _____ in an apartment.

11. He _____ 28 years old.

12. I _____ from New York.

E Read about Kenji.

Kenji Nakamura
Kenji is a student. He lives in Los Angeles. He is 22 years old. He is single.

F Write paragraphs about Anya and Gilberto from Exercise A.

Anya

_____

_____

_____

_____

_____

Gilberto

_____

_____

_____

_____

_____

G Complete the chart about your classmates.

Name	Marital status	Age	Residence

Everyday Life

CHALLENGE 2 ➤ Simple Present: *Have*

Simple Present: *Have*

A Read about Lien.

My name is Lien Nguyen. I have a wonderful family. Today, we live in the United States. I have three sisters and one brother. One of my sisters still lives in Vietnam. I also have aunts and an uncle here. My mother has three sisters, and she doesn't have brothers. My father has one brother and one sister.

B Answer the questions about Lien's family.

1. How many sisters does she have? _____

2. How many uncles does she have? _____

3. How many aunts does she have? _____

4. Where is she from? _____

5. Where do her father and mother live? _____

6. What's Lien's last name? _____

C Read the charts.

Simple Present: *Have*			
Subject	***Have***	**Information**	**Example sentence**
I, you, we, they	have	three brothers	I **have** three brothers.
		two sisters	We **have** two sisters.
he, she	has	no cousins	He **has** no cousins.
		three sons	She **has** three sons.

Negative: *Have*				
Subject	**Negative**	***Have***	**Information**	**Example Sentence**
I, you, we, they	don't	have	three brothers	I **don't have** three brothers.
			two sisters	We **don't have** three sisters.
he, she	doesn't		cousins	He **doesn't have** cousins.
			three sons	She **doesn't have** three sons.

D Circle the correct sentence.

1. (I have two sisters.) / I has two sisters.

2. I doesn't have a wife. / I don't have a wife.

3. You don't have an aunt in Korea. / They doesn't have uncles in the United States.

4. Ken have a brother. / Ken doesn't have a brother.

5. My mother have four sisters. / My mother has four sisters.

6. You doesn't have a niece in Poland. / You don't have a niece in Poland.

7. Maria doesn't have a husband. / Maria don't have a husband.

8. We doesn't have children. / We don't have children.

9. Jessica and Kate has a brother. / Jessica and Kate have a brother.

E Look at the diagram.

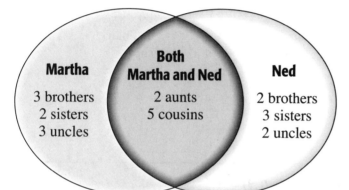

Martha

3 brothers
2 sisters
3 uncles

**Both
Martha and Ned**

2 aunts
5 cousins

Ned

2 brothers
3 sisters
2 uncles

F Write sentences using the information in Exercise E.

1. Martha has three brothers. _____

2. _____

3. _____

4. _____

5. _____

6. _____

G Write about you and a classmate.

I _____   My classmate _____

_____   _____

_____   _____

_____   _____

Everyday Life

CHALLENGE 3 ➤ Comparative and Superlative Adjectives

A Look at the three men.

6 feet
4 inches

5 feet
11 inches

5 feet
6 inches

Howard
green eyes
blond hair
tall

Sam
brown eyes
brown hair
average height

Kyle
blue eyes
red hair
short

B Write about the men in Exercise A.

Howard 1. Howard is tall.

2. He has blond hair and green eyes.

Sam 3. _____

4. _____

Kyle 5. _____

6. _____

C Read the chart.

Comparative and Superlative Adjectives		
Adjective	**Comparative adjectives**	**Superlative adjectives**
tall	taller (Steve is **taller than** Dalva.)	tallest
short	shorter (Dalva is **shorter than** Kenji.)	shortest
heavy	heavier (Gilberto is **heavier than** Lien.)	heaviest
thin	thinner (Marie is **thinner than** Sung.)	thinnest
old	older (Anya is **older than** Ahmed.)	oldest
young	younger (Mario is **younger than** Steve.)	youngest

D **Complete the sentences with comparative adjectives.**

1. John is _____taller_____ (tall) than Oscar.

2. Cynthia is _____ (short) than Oscar.

3. Herbert is _____ (heavy) than Huyen.

4. Lien is _____ (thin) than Huyen.

5. Jack is _____ (young) than Leti.

6. Frank is _____ (old) than Leti.

7. Kim is _____ (thin) than Jim and _____ (tall) than Karen.

8. Maria is _____ (tall) and _____ (thin) than Kim.

E **Answer the questions about Exercise D.**

1. Who is the tallest, Oscar, Cynthia, or John? _____

2. Who is heavier, Herbert or Huyen? _____

3. Who is heavier, Herbert or Lien? _____

4. Who is the thinnest, Herbert, Lien, or Huyen? _____

5. Who is the youngest, Jack, Leti, or Frank? _____

6. Who is the oldest, Jack, Leti, or Frank? _____

7. Who is the thinnest, Kim, Jim, or Maria? _____

F **Complete the chart about your class.**

	tall	taller	tallest
Names			
	short	shorter	shortest
Names			
	thin	thinner	thinnest
Names			

G **Write sentences about the class. Use the information from Exercise F.**

1. _____

2. _____

3. _____

Everyday Life

CHALLENGE 4 ➤ Simple Present and Frequency Words

A Read Kim's calendar.

Monday	Tuesday	Wednesday	Thursday
15 7:00 A.M. go to school / 9:00 A.M. take a break / 12:30 P.M. go to work	**16** 7:00 A.M. watch kids / 10:00 A.M. go to the store / 12:30 P.M. go to work	**17** 7:00 A.M. go to school / 9:00 A.M. take a break / 12:30 P.M. go to work	**18** 7:00 A.M. watch kids / 9:00 A.M. study / 12:30 P.M. go to work
22 7:00 A.M. go to school / 9:00 A.M. take a break / 12:30 P.M. go to work	**23** 7:00 A.M. watch kids / 10:00 A.M. go to the store / 12:30 P.M. go to work	**24** 7:00 A.M. go to school / 9:00 A.M. take a break / 12:30 P.M. go to work	**25** 7:00 A.M. watch kids / 9:00 A.M. study / 12:30 P.M. go to work

B Circle the correct answer about the calendar in Exercise A.

1. What does Kim do Monday through Thursday?
   a. She goes to school.
   b. She goes to the store.
   c. She goes to work.

2. When does Kim watch the kids?
   a. She watches the kids on Tuesday and Thursday in the morning.
   b. She watches the kids on Tuesday and Thursday in the evening.
   c. She watches the kids every day.

3. How often does Kim go to the store?
   a. She goes to the store once a week.
   b. She goes to the store twice a week.
   c. She goes to the store in the morning.

C Read the chart.

Simple Present			
Subject	**Verb**	**Information**	**Example sentence**
I, you, we, they	eat	lunch	I always **eat** lunch at 4:00 P.M.
	go	to school	You often **go** to school at 8:00 A.M.
	help	with the children	We sometimes **help** with the children.
	play	soccer	They never **play** soccer on Saturday.
he, she	eats	lunch	He rarely **eats** lunch at 12:00 P.M.
	goes	to school	Nadia always **goes** to school early.
	helps	with the children	Gilberto never **helps** with the children.
	plays	soccer	She sometimes **plays** soccer on Friday.

D Rewrite each sentence with the new subject in parentheses.

1. I wake up at 6:00 A.M. (Anya)   Anya wakes up at 6:00 A.M.

2. Ivan gets up at 7:00 A.M. (you)   _____

3. We go to work at 8:00 A.M. (Ivan)   _____

4. Anya helps with the grandchildren. (they)   _____

5. Vladimir and Ziven play soccer. (we)   _____

6. You work in Los Angeles. (Ivan)   _____

7. The children go to school. (I)   _____

8. I take the children to the beach. (Anya)   _____

E Complete each sentence with the verb and frequency word in parentheses.

1. (wake up / often) Gilberto _____often wakes up_____ at 5:00 A.M.

2. (work / always) He _____ at his father's restaurant.

3. (take / sometimes) His children _____ the bus to school.

4. (play / often) His friends _____ soccer on Sunday.

5. (work / sometimes) On Mondays, she _____ overtime.

6. (get up / rarely) I _____ at 6:00 A.M.

7. (wake up / sometimes) My brother _____ at 7:00 A.M.

8. (take / rarely) We _____ the bus to work.

F Write sentences about Exercise A.

1. Kim works every day at 12:30 P.M._____

2. _____

3. _____

4. _____

5. _____

6. _____

G In a group, talk about what you do every day.

Everyday Life

CHALLENGE 5 ➤ *Yes/No* Questions: *Is it?*

A Look at the weather pictures and read the labels.

Havana is hot and sunny.

Montreal is cold and sunny.

Tokyo is cloudy.

Lisbon is foggy.

B Practice the conversation with information from Exercise A.

Student A: How's the weather in Havana?
Student B: It's sunny.
Student A: Is it cold?
Student B: No, it isn't. It's hot.

C Read the chart.

		Yes/No Questions: *Is it?*	Answer	
Question + verb	Information	Question	Yes	No
Is it	hot	Is it hot outside?	Yes, it is.	No, it isn't.
	windy	Is it windy today?		
	cloudy	Is it cloudy in Florida?		
	rainy	Is it rainy there?		
	snowy	Is it snowy in the mountains?		
	cold	Is it cold in Chicago?		
	foggy	Is it foggy in the morning?		

D Change the statements to questions.

1. It is rainy today.

   <u>Is it rainy today?</u>

2. It is snowy in the mountains and a beautiful day.

   _____

3. It is hot and 96 degrees in California today.

   _____

4. It is foggy by the ocean every morning.

   _____

5. It's windy at night.

   _____

6. It's cloudy and rainy today.

   _____

E Read the weather forecast.

Sunday		Monday		Tuesday		Wednesday		Thursday	
sunny		windy		windy		cloudy		rainy	
High:	80°	High:	72°	High:	74°	High:	68°	High:	63°
Low:	65°	Low:	62°	Low:	60°	Low:	56°	Low:	52°

F Answer the questions with short answers.

1. Today is Thursday. Is it sunny? <u>No, it isn't.</u>

2. Today is Sunday. Is the high 80 degrees? _____

3. Today is Tuesday. Is it windy? _____

4. Today is Sunday. Is it sunny? _____

5. It is Monday morning. Is it 60 degrees? _____

6. Today is Wednesday. Is it cloudy? _____

G Write two true statements and two false statements about the weather today.

True: _____

True: _____

False: _____

False: _____

H Ask a classmate *yes/no* questions about your statements in Exercise G.

UNIT 1 Everyday Life

EXTENSION CHALLENGE 1 ➤ Negative Statements with *Be*

A Read the paragraphs.

Mario Gutierrez

My name is Mario Gutierrez. I am from Michoacan, Mexico. I am single. I am a student in an adult school in Los Angeles. I am 28 years old. I have black hair and brown eyes. I am not tall. I am short. I go to school every day. I want to learn English. I am a little nervous in class, but I participate because it is important.

Sylvia Rodriguez

My name is Sylvia Rodriguez. I am not from Mexico. I am from Peru. I am single. I am a student in an adult school in Los Angeles. I am 26 years old. I have black hair and brown eyes. I am considered to be of average height. Sometimes I go to school. I work every day. I want to learn English. I am happy here in the United States.

B Complete the chart about Mario and Sylvia.

Name	Marital status	Native country	Height	Eye color	Hair color
Mario					
Sylvia					

C Read the chart.

Negative Statements with *Be*				
Subject	Negative *be*	Information	Contracted forms	
I	**am not**	nervous.	I'm **not**	—
You	**are not**	in Houston.	you're **not**	you **aren't**
He, She, It	**is not**	short.	he's, she's, it's **not**	he, she, it **isn't**
We	**are not**	hungry.	we're **not**	we **aren't**
They	**are not**	from Korea.	they're **not**	they **aren't**

• There is only one contracted form for *I am not: I'm not.*

• There are two contracted forms for the other negative forms of *be.*

D Bubble in the correct word or words to complete each sentence. Fill in the bubble completely.

1. I _____ at work on Monday. ○ isn't   ● am not
2. I _____ at school on Tuesday. ○ 'm not   ○ 's not
3. It _____ sunny this afternoon. ○ 're not   ○ 's not
4. It _____ very warm either. ○ isn't   ○ aren't
5. My friends _____ at the beach today. ○ are not   ○ is not
6. They _____ happy about the weather. ○ isn't   ○ aren't
7. We _____ always busy. ○ 's not   ○ 're not
8. We _____ tired either. ○ are not   ○ am not
9. My friend Mario _____ single. ○ is not   ○ are not
10. My friend Lien _____ married. ○ 're not   ○ 's not

E Use the words in parentheses and make each sentence negative. Use a contraction.

1. Mario is from Mexico. (Peru). _____ Mario isn't from Peru. _____

2. Her name is Sylvia. (Maria). _____

3. They are students. (teachers) _____

4. His last name is Gutierrez. (Ortiz) _____

5. Sylvia is happy in the U.S. (sad) _____

6. Mario is short. (tall) _____

7. Sylvia and Mario are single. (married) _____

8. Sylvia is young. (old) _____

F Complete the sentences about you.

1. I'm a student. _____ I'm not a teacher. _____

2. I'm _____. I'm not _____

3. My classmate is _____. _____

4. My parents are _____. _____

UNIT **1** **Everyday Life**

EXTENSION CHALLENGE 2 ➤ *Yes/No Questions with Be*

Yes/No Quetions with Be

A Read John's delivery schedule.

Monday	Tuesday	Wednesday	Thursday
15 Los Angeles	16 Anaheim Newport Beach	17 Long Beach Orange	18 San Clemente San Juan
22 Los Angeles	23 Anaheim	24 Long Beach	25 San Juan

B Answer the questions about where John's meetings are each day by circling *Yes* or *No*.

1. Is John in Anaheim on the sixteenth? — (Yes)   No
2. Is John in San Clemente and Anaheim on Thursday? — Yes   No
3. Where is John on Monday, in Los Angeles? — Yes   No
4. Is John in Long Beach on Tuesday? — Yes   No
5. Is John in Santa Ana on Wednesday? — Yes   No
6. Where else is John on Tuesday, Anaheim? — Yes   No

C Read the chart.

			Yes/No Questions with Be	
Be	**Subject**	**Information**	**Example question**	**Short answer**
am	I	happy	**Am** I happy?	Yes, I am. / No, I'm not.
are	you	married	**Are** you married?	Yes, you are. / No, you're not.
	we	friends	**Are** we friends?	Yes, we are. / No, we're not.
	they	brothers	**Are** they brothers?	Yes, they are. / No, they're not.
is	he	from Italy	**Is** he from Italy?	Yes, he is. / No, he's not.
	she	in class today	**Is** she in class today?	Yes, she is. / No, she's not.
	it	sunny today	**Is** it sunny today?	Yes, it is. / No, it's not.

D Use the words to ask a *yes/no* question.

1. Kenji / from Japan   <u>   Is Kenji from Japan?   </u>

2. Anya and Ivan / from Russia   <u>   </u>

3. you / from Korea   <u>   </u>

4. I / late for class   <u>   </u>

5. Marie / from Haiti   <u>   </u>

6. Gilberto and Mario / tall   <u>   </u>

7. Mario / from Mexico   <u>   </u>

8. Kenji / at school   <u>   </u>

E Read the chart.

Kenji	Anya	Gilberto	Marie
single	married	single	divorced
22 years old	68 years old	30 years old	32 years old
Los Angeles	Los Angeles	Los Angeles	Los Angeles

F Using the chart in Exercise E, answer the questions with short answers.

1. Is Kenji married? <u>   No, he's not.   </u>

2. Are Gilberto and Kenji single? <u>   </u>

3. Is Anya single? <u>   </u>

4. Are Marie and Anya in Los Angeles? <u>   </u>

5. Are Marie and Kenji married? <u>   </u>

6. Is Anya young? <u>   </u>

7. Is Marie 32 years old? <u>   </u>

G Ask classmates *yes/no* questions to complete the chart.

Name	Marital status	Native country	Height	Eye color	Hair color

UNIT 2 Let's go shopping!

CHALLENGE 1 ➤ Negative and Affirmative Simple Present

A Look at the clothing words.

sandals	a scarf	shorts	boots
a t-shirt	a jacket	a sweater	sunglasses
a cap	a dress	a coat	a swimsuit

B Complete the chart with the words in Exercise A.

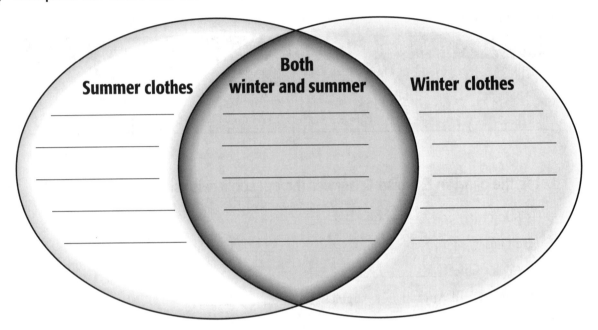

Summer clothes

Both winter and summer

Winter clothes

C Read the charts.

Affirmative Simple Present		
I	wear	
you	like	
we	want	
they	need	
		shoes
	wears	
he	likes	
she	wants	
	needs	

Negative Simple Present			
I			
you	do not	wear	
we	(don't)	like	
they			sandals
		want	
he	does not	need	
she	(doesn't)		

D Complete each sentence with the negative form of the underlined verb.

1. Kenji <u>shops</u> at Bayview Mall. He _____doesn't shop_____ at Maple Lake Mall.

2. Marie <u>wears</u> sandals to the beach. She _____ sandals to work.

3. I <u>need</u> jeans for my work. I _____ a suit.

4. You <u>buy</u> shoes at Allen's Shoe Store. You _____ shoes at The Shoe Place.

5. My parents <u>like</u> the new mall. They _____ the old mall.

6. Ivan <u>needs</u> new boots. He _____ new shoes.

7. You often <u>shop</u> on Saturday. You _____ on Sunday.

8. After shopping, we always <u>eat</u> in the mall. We _____ at home.

9. Tan and Diem <u>want</u> new summer clothes. They _____ new winter clothes.

10. I <u>work</u> in a small store. I _____ in a department store.

E Complete the sentences with information from Exercise B.

1. I _____wear_____ (wear-*affirmative*) a jacket in the winter.

   I _____don't wear_____ (wear-*negative*) a t-shirt.

2. He _____ (like-*affirmative*) a scarf in the winter.

   He _____ (like-*negative*) shorts.

3. We _____ (need-*affirmative*) boots in the winter.

   We _____ (need-*negative*) sandals.

4. She _____ (want-*affirmative*) shorts in the summer.

   She _____ (want-*negative*) pants.

5. You _____ (wear-*affirmative*) a jacket in the winter.

   You _____ (wear-*negative*) a swimsuit.

F Complete the chart with clothing you wear at home and at work.

Home		Work	

G Talk to a classmate about Exercise F.

Negative and Affirmative Simple Present

Unit 2   **17**

UNIT 2

Let's go shopping!

CHALLENGE 2 ➤ Comparative and Superlative Adjectives

A Read the price for each item.

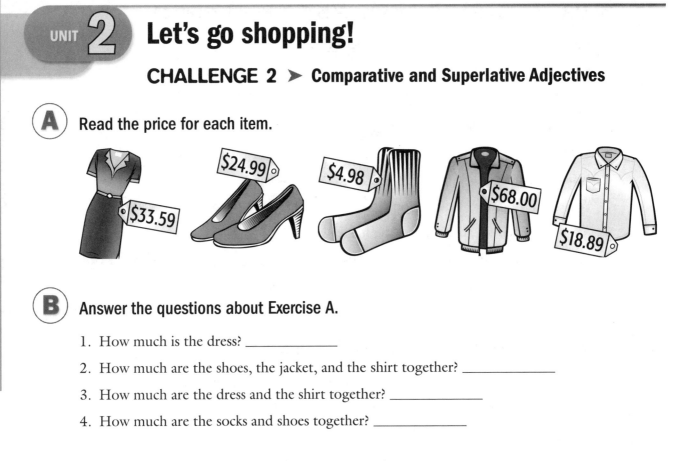

$33.59 $24.99 $4.98 $68.00 $18.89

B Answer the questions about Exercise A.

1. How much is the dress? _____

2. How much are the shoes, the jacket, and the shirt together? _____

3. How much are the dress and the shirt together? _____

4. How much are the socks and shoes together? _____

C Put the clothing from Exercise A in order from cheap to expensive.

cheap ———————————————————➤ expensive

_____socks_____ _____ _____ _____ _____

D Read the chart.

Adjective	Comparative adjective	Example sentence
cheap	cheaper	The shirt is **cheaper** *than* the dress.
expensive	more expensive	The shoes are **more expensive** *than* the shirt.
	less expensive	The dress is **less expensive** *than* the jacket.

Adjective	Superlatives	Example sentence
cheap	cheapest	The socks are the **cheapest**.
expensive	most expensive	The jacket is the **most expensive**.
	least expensive	The socks are the **least expensive**.

E Read the price tags and complete the sentences with the comparative or the superlative.

1. The pants are _____cheaper than_____ the sweater.

2. The shorts are _____ the sandals.

3. The sweater is _____ the pajamas.

4. The pants are _____ the sandals.

5. The sandals are the _____.

6. The sweater is the _____.

7. The sandals and the shorts together are _____ than the sweater.

8. The pajamas and the sandals together are _____ the sweater and the pants.

F Put the clothing from Exercises A and E in order from cheap to expensive.

cheap ──→ expensive

socks									

G Look at the clothing on pages 18 and 19. Complete the sentences.

1. The sweater is cheaper than _____.

2. _____ are each more expensive than a dress.

3. _____ are the least expensive.

4. _____ is the most expensive.

5. _____ are less expensive than the _____.

6. _____ are cheaper than _____.

H In a group, choose five items of clothing (different from this challenge). What are the prices? What is the cheapest and the most expensive?

cheapest ──→ most expensive

Let's go shopping!

CHALLENGE 3 ➤ Present Continuous

A Read the inventory list.

Washington Fine Clothing

Item number	Size	Color / pattern	Item	Retail unit price	Quantity
015534-B	S	blue	short-sleeved shirt	$24.50	28
015534-W	S	white	short-sleeved shirt	$24.50	15
015655-B	S	blue/striped	long-sleeved shirt	$24.50	18
025533-Br	M	brown	long-sleeved shirt	$44.98	2
025531-B	M	blue/flowered	long-sleeved shirt	$32.95	31
035573-Br	L	brown	short-sleeved shirt	$35.75	7
045521-G	XL	green	short-sleeved shirt	$45.99	5

B Practice the conversation with information from the inventory above.

Customer: Excuse me. How much are the <u>large, brown, short-sleeved</u> shirts?
Salesperson: They are <u>$35.75</u> each.
Customer: Thanks. Is that before tax?
Salesperson: That's right, before tax.

C Read the charts.

Affirmative Present Continuous			
Subject	***Be***	**Base + *ing***	
I	am	wearing	right now
you, we, they	are	buying going	at this moment
he, she, it	is	shopping eating	today

Negative Present Continuous				
Subject	***Be***	***not***	**Base + *ing***	
I (I'm)	am	not	waiting buying	right now
you, we, they	are	not (aren't)	going	at this moment
he, she, it	is	not (isn't)	shopping eating	today

D Fill in the missing part of each sentence.

1. It's rain _ing_ today.
2. Marie isn't work____ today.
3. She ____ going with us.
4. I'm wear____ my raincoat.
5. We ____ wearing hats.
6. Anya and Ivan ____ shopping today.
7. They ____ buying winter clothes.
8. Mario ____ working today.
9. Teresa is work____ right now.
10. They ____n't going to the mall.

E Use the words to write sentences in the present continuous.

EXAMPLE: many people / shop / today   _____Many people are shopping today._____

1. Anya / look / for new summer clothes   _____
2. I / buy / sandals   _____
3. you / wear / your new blouse   _____
4. three men / sit / on a bench   _____
5. we / not / eat / at the mall today   _____
6. Duong / go / to the shoe store   _____
7. the children / talk / to their friends   _____
8. Irina / not / buy the blue skirt   _____
9. you / read / a book at the bookstore   _____
10. we / take / the bus home   _____

F Imagine that you are talking to a friend on the phone. Have a phone conversation about what you are wearing. Use the information from Exercise A.

EXAMPLE:
Student A: Hi, John. What are you wearing?
Student B: I am wearing a small, blue, short-sleeved shirt.
Student A: What is your wife wearing?
Student B: She's wearing a small, white, short-sleeved shirt.

G Select three classmates and ask them to describe what they are wearing. List in the chart below. Then, describe what they are wearing to a partner.

Name	Size	Color / pattern	Style	Item

Let's go shopping!

CHALLENGE 4 ➤ Using *Because*

A Read the graph.

Comparison Shopping

□ Armstrong Clothing
■ Fashion Express

B Answer the questions.

1. Where is it cheaper to buy women's shoes? _____

2. Where is it cheaper to buy women's belts? _____

3. Where is it more expensive to buy handbags? _____

4. Where is it more expensive to buy women's shoes? _____

5. Where is it more expensive to buy dresses? _____

C Talk in a group. Estimate the prices.

	Shoes	Dresses	Handbags	Belts
Armstrong Clothing	$35.00			
Fashion Express	$39.00			

D Read the chart.

Using *Because*			
Statement	*Because*	Reason Subject + verb	Example sentence
I want the blue shirt	because	it is cheaper	I want the blue shirt **because** it is cheaper.
I shop at Addy's	because	it is close	I shop at Addy's **because** it is close to my home.
You like the shirt	because	it is green	You like the shirt **because** it is green.

E **Match the statement with the reason.**

1. I like Armstrong's.   a. The dress is long and beautiful.
2. I want the dress.   b. The shoes are cheap.
3. I like the shoes.   c. The blouses are cheaper than at Fashion Express.
4. I want the hat.   d. The pants are my size.
5. I like the shirt.   e. The shirt has long sleeves.
6. I want the pants.   f. The hat is perfect with my dress.

F **Combine the statements and the reasons in Exercise E with** *because*.

EXAMPLE: <u>I like Armstrong's because the blouses are cheaper than at Fashion Express.</u>

1. _____
2. _____
3. _____
4. _____
5. _____
6. _____

G **Read the paragraph.**

   Kim shops at Sally's Clothing Store because it has good prices. The store has good salespeople. Sally's Clothing Store has a great selection for women. The store is on First and Main downtown. Kim likes the shoes. They are cheaper than at other stores.

H **Write sentences using** *because* **to answer the questions.**

1. Why does Kim like Sally's Clothing Store?
   <u>Kim likes Sally's Clothing Store because it has good prices.</u>

2. What is another reason she likes the store? (good salespeople)

   _____

3. What is another reason she likes the store? (great selection)

   _____

4. Why does Kim like the shoes?

   _____

I **Talk to a classmate about your favorite store. Use** *because* **to say why.**

Let's go shopping!

UNIT 2

CHALLENGE 5 ➤ Demonstrative Adjectives: *this, that, these,* and *those*

A Read the information.

I don't like the color.	It doesn't fit. (They don't fit.)
I don't like it. (I don't like them.)	It is the wrong size. (They are the wrong size.)
It is damaged. (They are damaged.)	

1. Roberto
   Item: these jeans
   Problem: size

2. Gilberto
   Item: this shirt
   Problem: color

3. Janet
   Item: these shoes
   Problem: color

4. Marie
   Item: this dress
   Problem: damaged

5. Lien
   Item: these socks
   Problem: damaged

6. Alexi
   Item: these shorts
   Problem: size

B Read the conversation.

Manager: May I help you?
Roberto: Yes, I want to return <u>these jeans</u>.
Manager: OK, what's the problem?
Roberto: <u>They don't fit</u>.

C Practice the conversation in Exercise B. Use information from Exercise A.

D Read the chart.

Demonstrative Adjectives: *this, that, these, those*		
	Near	**Far**
Singular	this sweater this hat	that sweater that hat
Plural	these shoes these pants	those shoes those pants
Example sentences		
	Near	**Far**
Singular	This sweater is perfect. I want **this** hat.	That sweater is blue. I like **that** hat.
Plural	These pants fit. I like **these** shoes.	Those pants are great! I like **those** shoes.

E **Read each sentence. Are the underlined words *singular* or *plural*, *near* or *far*? Mark two boxes for each sentence.**

	Singular	Plural	Near	Far
1. <u>Those apples</u> are delicious.	☐	■	☐	■
2. Are <u>those belts</u> expensive?	☐	☐	☐	☐
3. How much is <u>that t-shirt</u>?	☐	☐	☐	☐
4. What color are <u>these ties</u>?	☐	☐	☐	☐
5. Is <u>that dress</u> new?	☐	☐	☐	☐
6. <u>These apples</u> are green.	☐	☐	☐	☐
7. <u>This vacuum cleaner</u> is heavy.	☐	☐	☐	☐
8. I don't like <u>those jeans</u>.	☐	☐	☐	☐

F **Use *this, that, these, those*, and the information in parentheses to complete the sentences.**

1. (near) Look at _____this_____ shirt. It is perfect for school.

2. (near) I want to return _____ shoes. They don't fit.

3. (far) _____ pants are the wrong size.

4. (near) I like _____ scarf. It is beautiful.

5. (far) _____ shorts are very colorful.

6. (far) _____ socks are not my size.

7. (near) I want to return _____ radio.

8. (far) _____ books are interesting.

9. (far) _____ cars are new.

10. (near) We need _____ gloves for the winter.

G **You need to return some things to the store. Write a conversation and perform it for the class.**

Student A: _____

Student B: _____

Student A: _____

Student B: _____

Student A: _____

Student B: _____

UNIT **2**

Let's go shopping!

EXTENSION CHALLENGE 1 ➤ **Simple Present: Yes/No Questions**

A Look at Lien and Steve.

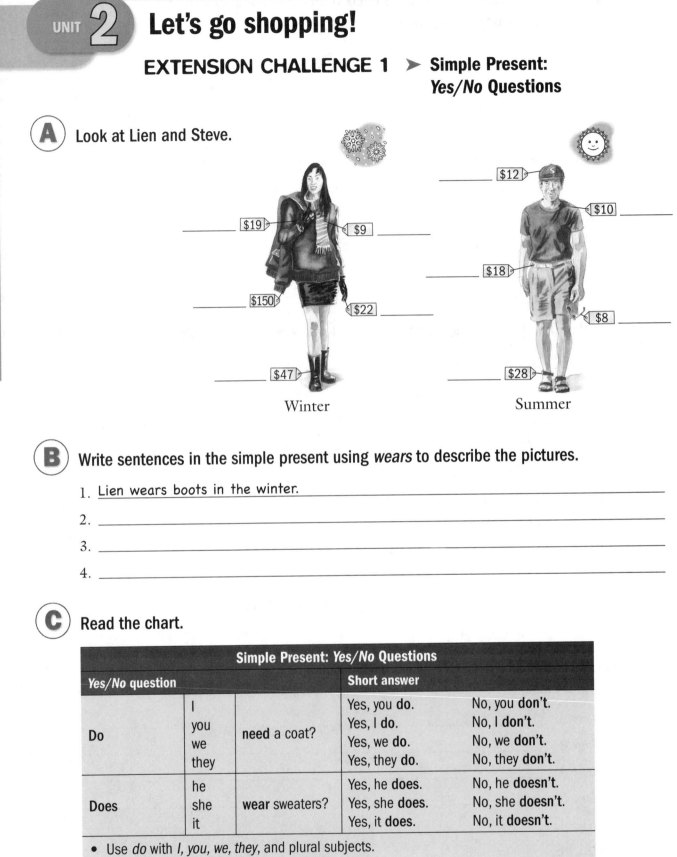

$12

$19 $9

$10

$150 $18

$22 $8

$47 $28

Winter   Summer

B Write sentences in the simple present using *wears* to describe the pictures.

1. Lien wears boots in the winter.

2. _____

3. _____

4. _____

C Read the chart.

Simple Present: *Yes/No Questions*				
Yes/No question			**Short answer**	
Do	I you we they	**need** a coat?	Yes, you **do**. Yes, I **do**. Yes, we **do**. Yes, they **do**.	No, you **don't**. No, I **don't**. No, we **don't**. No, they **don't**.
Does	he she it	**wear** sweaters?	Yes, he **does**. Yes, she **does**. Yes, it **does**.	No, he **doesn't**. No, she **doesn't**. No, it **doesn't**.

- Use *do* with *I, you, we, they,* and plural subjects.
- Use *does* with *he, she, it,* and singular subjects.
- Always use the base form after *do* or *does*.

D Read each statement. Write a *yes/no* question using that statement.

EXAMPLE: You like my shoes. _____Do you like my shoes?_____

1. They cost $45.00. _____

2. The price includes tax. _____

3. You shop at the mall. _____

4. Kenji shops there, too. _____

5. We want to buy new clothes. _____

6. I need more money. _____

7. Mr. Lee has a new raincoat. _____

8. Silvia wears sandals every day. _____

E Answer each question according to the information in parentheses.

EXAMPLE: Does Lien wear boots in the winter? (yes) _____Yes, she does._____

1. Do you use coupons? (yes) _____

2. Does the ad give the regular price? (no) _____

3. Does Addy's Clothing Store have good prices? (yes) _____

4. Do Mario and Teresa shop at Addy's Clothing Store? (no) _____

5. Do we have $75.00 for the coat? (no) _____

6. Does the price include tax? (yes) _____

7. Do I need a coat today? (yes) _____

8. Does Alexi buy cheap shoes? (no) _____

9. Do you have $25.00? (no) _____

10. Does your mother need a new hat? (yes) _____

F Look at Lien and Steve in Exercise A. Ask a partner what they wear in the summer and in the winter.

EXAMPLE: Does Lien wear sandals in the winter?

G Ask what a partner wears to school. Use *yes/no* questions. Check the answers (✓) .

☐ boots   ☐ a t-shirt   ☐ a jacket

☐ tennis shoes   ☐ shorts   ☐ sandals

☐ gloves   ☐ glasses   ☐ a hat

UNIT 2 Let's go shopping!

EXTENSION CHALLENGE 2 ➤ Present Continuous: Yes/No Questions

A Read the paragraph.

Irina, her husband Alexi, and their daughter Larissa are from Russia. They live in New York City. They want to buy clothes for work and for school. They are looking at a flyer to see what people are wearing. They are talking about the clothing.

Come shop our 50 stores!

MOUNTAIN VIEW MALL

Men's and Women's Career Wear

School Clothing

Teen's Dress and Casual Clothing

Men's and Women's Work Clothing

B Describe to a partner what people are wearing in the flyer.

C Read the chart.

Present Continuous: *Yes/No* Questions				
Be	Subject	Base verb + *ing*	Short answer	
Am	I	**going** with you to the mall?	Yes, you **are**.	No, you **aren't**.
Are	you	**shopping** today?	Yes, I **am**.	No, I'm **not**.
Is	he, she, it	**wearing** a sweater?	Yes, he/she/it **is**.	No, he/she/it **isn't**.
Are	we	**buying** new jeans now?	Yes, we **are**.	No, we **aren't**.
Are	they	**having** a sale right now?	Yes, they **are**.	No, they **aren't**.

D **Ask *yes/no* questions about what these people are buying.**

EXAMPLE: Diem / the striped shirt   Is Diem buying the striped shirt?

1. Anya and Ivan / summer clothes   _____

2. you / the blue pants or the red pants _____

3. I / the dress with a coupon   _____

4. Teresa / the flowered raincoat   _____

5. we / the extra-large t-shirts   _____

6. they / expensive shoes   _____

7. Steve / the brown boots   _____

8. your family / winter clothes today   _____

E **Answer each question according to the information in parentheses.**

EXAMPLE: Is he using a discount coupon? (yes)   Yes, he is.

1. Are they looking at the clothing in a flyer? (yes) _____

2. Is he saving $10 with the coupon? (no)   _____

3. Are you buying the skirt for $39.95? (yes)   _____

4. Is Lien buying the dress at the regular price? (no) _____

5. Am I saving $5 with the coupon? (no)   _____

6. Are we taking the receipt? (yes)   _____

7. Are the children buying new backpacks? (yes)   _____

8. Are you reading the advertisement? (no)   _____

F **Look at the pictures and write *yes/no* questions.**

1   2   3   4

1. Are they wearing suits? _____

2. _____

3. _____

4. _____

Food and Nutrition

CHALLENGE 1 ➤ Questions with *Can*

A Read the menu.

Edgar's Kitchen

SOUPS AND SALADS

Split Pea soup $1.99
Wonton soup $1.99
Caesar salad $2.49
Dinner salad $1.99

SIDE ORDERS

French fries $1.49
Potato chips .... $.99
Onion rings $1.49
Baked potato $1.25

MAIN DISHES

SANDWICHES

Ham and cheese...................$3.99
Tuna $3.99
Roast beef $4.29
Hamburger $3.49

DISHES

Roast beef with whipped $7.49
    potatoes and vegetable
Teriyaki chicken with $5.99
    rice and vegetable
Beef and broccoli...................$4.99
    with fried rice
Sirloin steak with $8.99
    baked potato and vegetable

DESSERTS

Vanilla ice cream $2.49
Carrot cake $2.49
Apple pie $2.49

BEVERAGES

Sodas .... $.99
Milk $1.29
Coffee $1.29
Tea $1.29

B Answer the questions about the menu.

1. What is the most expensive item on the menu? _____ sirloin steak _____

2. What are the cheapest items on the menu? _____

3. What is your favorite sandwich on the menu? _____

4. What is your favorite main dish on the menu? _____

5. How much is the total for a dinner salad, a sirloin steak dish, and milk? _____

C Read the chart.

Can	Subject	Base verb	Example sentence
Questions with *Can*			
can	I		Can I take your order? Can I help you?
can	you	take help	Can you take my order? Can you take our order, please? Can you help me? Can you help us?

D Write questions with the words provided.

1. I / can / take / your dishes _____ Can I take your dishes? _____

2. help / me / understand / can / you _____

3. you / see / can / the server _____

4. you / can / eat / faster _____

5. I / can / talk to the manager _____

6. pay / can / you _____

7. I / have / can / the shrimp _____

8. help / you / can _____

E Match each statement with a question.

1. I need the server.   a. Can I have the dinner salad?

2. I want the dinner salad.   b. Can I speak to the manager?

3. I need the manager!   c. Can you see the server?

4. I finished my dinner.   d. Can I take your dishes?

F Write questions.

1. I need a soda. Can I have a soda, please? _____

2. I want to talk to the manager. _____

3. You need to help me. _____

4. You can take my dishes. _____

G Take an order from a partner. Use the menu in Exercise A.

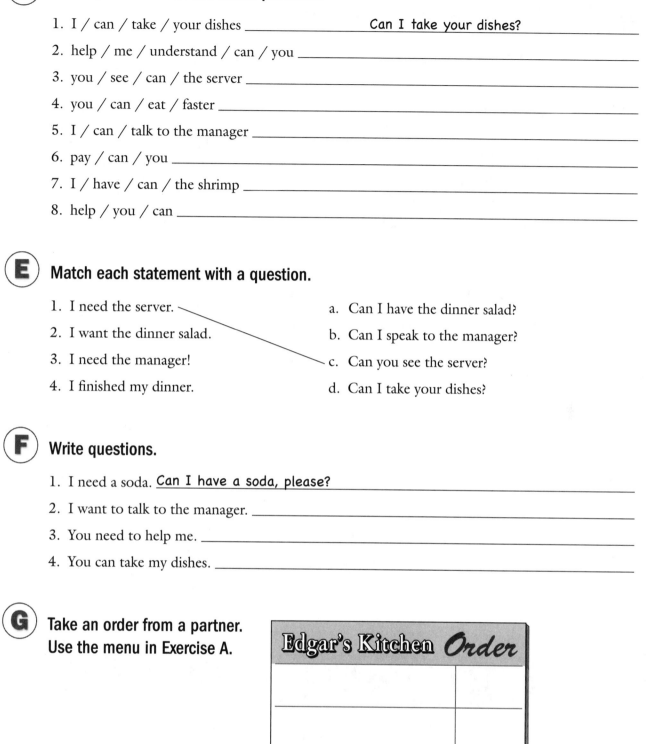

Edgar's Kitchen Order

Total

UNIT 3 Food and Nutrition

CHALLENGE 2 ➤ *How much / How many*

A Look at the shopping lists.

Jose
- 3 pounds of bananas
- 2 gallons of milk
- 1 loaf of bread
- 1 jar of peanut butter
- 2 boxes of cereal
- 3 bags of potato chips

Marie
- 2 pounds of oranges
- 1 can of green beans
- 1 loaf of bread
- 2 gallons of milk
- 1 carton of ice cream
- 1 bottle of oil

B Complete the diagram about the shopping lists.

Jose   Both   Marie

C Read the chart.

How much / How many	
Count nouns	**Noncount nouns**
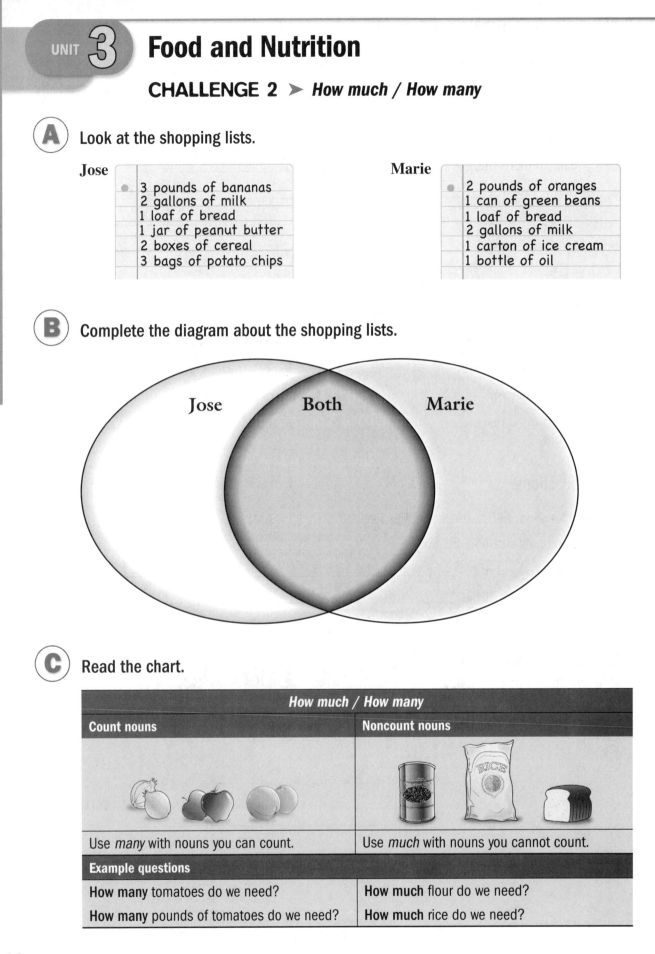	
Use *many* with nouns you can count.	Use *much* with nouns you cannot count.
Example questions	
How many tomatoes do we need?	**How much** flour do we need?
How many pounds of tomatoes do we need?	**How much** rice do we need?

D **Put the words in the correct column.**

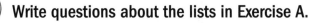

bottles	oil	ice cream	cartons
gallons of milk	jars	milk	soup
cans of soup	water	pounds of potatoes	bread

How much	*How many*
	bottles

E **Write questions about the lists in Exercise A.**

1. How many pounds of bananas do we need? _____

2. How much bread do we need? _____

3. How much _____

4. How many _____

5. How many _____

6. How much _____

7. How many _____

8. How much _____

9. How much _____

10. How many _____

F **You are having a party for 50 people. What do you need? Make a shopping list. Work in a group.**

hamburger buns
pickles
lettuce
ground beef
cheese
tomatoes
onions
potato chips
soda

CHALLENGE 3 ➤ Questions and Answers with *Be*

Questions and Answers with *Be*

A Read the signs in the supermarket. Complete the chart by listing two or more items you might expect to find in each aisle.

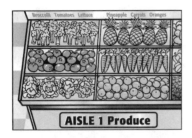

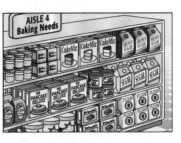

Aisle 1: Produce	Aisle 4: Baking Needs	Aisle 8: Meats
pears, oranges, tomatoes		

Aisle 3: Canned Goods	Aisle 5: Dairy/Frozen Foods	

B Read the charts.

<table>
<tr><th colspan="3">Questions with Be</th></tr>
<tr><th>Question word</th><th>Be</th><th>Singular or Plural</th></tr>
<tr><td>Where</td><td>is</td><td>the milk?
the water?
the oil?</td></tr>
<tr><td>Where</td><td>are</td><td>the eggs?
the bananas?
the pears?</td></tr>
</table>

<table>
<tr><th colspan="3">Answers with Be</th></tr>
<tr><th>Subject</th><th>Be</th><th>Location</th></tr>
<tr><td>The milk
It</td><td>is</td><td>in Aisle 1.</td></tr>
<tr><td>The eggs
They</td><td>are</td><td>in Aisle 5.</td></tr>
</table>

C. Bubble in the correct form.

1. Where _____ the potato chips?　　○ is　● are
2. Where _____ the soup?　　○ is　○ are
3. Where _____ the milk?　　○ is　○ are
4. Where _____ the bread?　　○ is　○ are
5. Where _____ the cake mix?　　○ is　○ are
6. Where _____ the oranges?　　○ is　○ are
7. Where _____ the chicken?　　○ is　○ are
8. Where _____ the cookies?　　○ is　○ are
9. The peanut butter _____ in Aisle 3.　　○ is　○ are
10. The flour _____ in Aisle 4.　　○ is　○ are
11. The carrots _____ in the canned good section.　　○ is　○ are
12. The bread _____ in the bakery.　　○ is　○ are

D. Complete the chart with the missing questions and statements.

Questions	Answers
Where are the potatoes?	
Where is the cake mix?	
	The cheese is in Aisle 5.
Where are the pears?	
	The milk is in the dairy section.
Where is the flour?	
	The bread is in the bakery.
	The chicken is in the meat section.

E. Practice the conversation and substitute information from Exercise A.

Student A: Excuse me. Where <u>are the</u> <u>potatoes</u>?

Student B: They are in the produce section.

Student A: Where <u>is the</u> <u>produce section</u>?

Student B: It is in Aisle 1.

Student A: Thank you.

Food and Nutrition

CHALLENGE 4 ➤ Using *Have*

A Label the food groups with the words below.

Breads, grains	Fruit	~~Vegetables~~	Dairy	Meat	Fats, oils, sweets

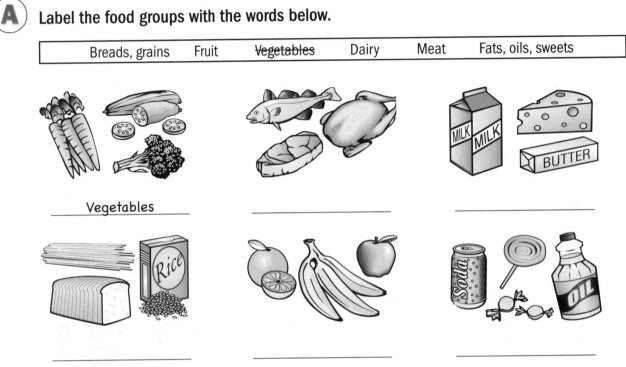

Vegetables _____   _____   _____

_____   _____   _____

B Name each of the food items in Exercise A.

C Read the chart.

Using *Have*			
Subject	**Have**	**Information**	**Example sentence**
I		cereal	I **have** cereal for breakfast.
you	have	pizza	You **have** pizza for dinner.
we		milk	We **have** milk with lunch.
they		eggs	They **have** eggs for breakfast.
he	has	soup	He **has** soup with dinner.
she		ice cream	She **has** ice cream for dessert.

D Write *have* or *has*.

1. John and Sylvia _____have_____ cereal for breakfast.

2. Nathan and I _____ steak for dinner.

3. You _____ breakfast every morning.

4. They _____ water with dinner every night.

5. I _____ a salad for lunch and a sandwich for dinner.

6. Gilberto _____ a piece of toast for breakfast.

7. She _____ a hamburger every day for lunch.

8. He _____ a donut for breakfast.

E Read the information.

Javier	Huyen	Alexi
Breakfast: a donut, milk	**Breakfast:** cereal, milk	**Breakfast:** fruit, milk
Lunch: a ham sandwich	**Lunch:** a ham sandwich	**Lunch:** a hamburger, fries
Dinner: a salad, soda	**Dinner:** chicken and rice	**Dinner:** chicken and rice

F Write sentences about the meals in Exercise E.

1. Javier <u>has a donut with milk for breakfast.</u> _____

2. Huyen and Javier _____

3. Alexi _____

4. Alexi and Huyen _____

5. _____

6. _____

7. _____

8. _____

G Complete the list of meals for you and a partner.

My Meals
Breakfast:
Lunch:
Dinner:

My Partner's Meals
Breakfast:
Lunch:
Dinner:

Food and Nutrition

UNIT

CHALLENGE 5 ➤ Imperatives

A Read the recipe.

Egg Salad Sandwiches

Serves 4 people

Ingredients	6 eggs	8 slices of bread
	2 tablespoons of mayonnaise	salt to taste
	1 tablespoon of mustard	
	lettuce	

Instructions	
❶	*Boil eggs.*
❷	
❸	
❹	
❺	
❻	
❼	
❽	

B Read the instructions below. They are in the wrong order. Number them in the correct order and then, fill in the "Instructions" section on the recipe card.

_____ Put eggs in cold water.

_____ Serve on bread.

__1__ Boil eggs.

_____ Finally, add salt and chopped lettuce.

_____ Mash eggs with a fork.

_____ Add mayonnaise and mustard.

_____ Peel eggs.

__6__ Mix ingredients.

C Read the charts.

Imperatives			
		Base verb	**Example sentence**
~~you~~		drain	**Drain** the water.
		chop	**Chop** the potatoes.
		peel	**Peel** the potatoes.
Negative Imperative			
		Base verb	**Example sentence**
~~you~~	do not	boil	**Don't boil** the water.
	don't	use	**Do not use** butter.
		cook	**Don't cook** in the microwave.

D Complete each sentence with a verb from the box. More than one answer is often possible.

read	listen	ask	don't put	~~help~~	write
don't use	don't eat	don't take	don't cook	cut	

EXAMPLE: __Help__ your sister make dinner.

1. _____ the server about the menu.
2. _____ the shopping list.
3. _____ my bowl.
4. _____ to your parents.
5. _____ eggs in the microwave.

6. _____ candy all day.
7. _____ the carrots in half.
8. _____ a check for the food.
9. _____ the dog to the restaurant.
10. _____ pennies in the vending machine.

E Read Silvia's instructions to her children. Use the imperatives.

__Don't watch__ (watch, *negative*) TV now. I need your help. Please _____ (1. vacuum) the rug and _____ (2. clean) your rooms. _____ (3. eat, *negative*) the snacks in the living room. _____ (4. buy) eggs, milk, and bread. _____ (5. buy, *negative*) the food at the convenience store. _____ (6. go) to Food City. _____ (7. peel) and _____ (8. whip) the potatoes. _____ (9. make) a salad. _____ (10. wash) and _____ (11. drain) the lettuce first. Then, _____ (12. set) the table. _____ (13. use, negative) the blue plates. Use the white plates. _____ (14. choose) some pretty napkins. _____ (15. put) on some nice clothes.

F Complete a favorite recipe. Use the imperative in the instructions. Use Exercise B for a model.

			Serves ___ people
Ingredients			
Instructions			

EXTENSION CHALLENGE 1 ➤ *Some/Any*

Some/Any

A Label the containers.

box _____

_____

_____

_____

_____

_____

B Complete Marvin's shopping list with the containers in Exercise A.

3 _____jars_____ of instant coffee
2 _____ of yogurt
1 _____ of cereal
1 _____ of oil
3 _____ of flour
2 _____ of soup

C Read the chart.

Some / Any		
	Count (Plural)	**Noncount**
Affirmative	I eat **some** vegetables every day.	I often eat **some** rice for dinner.
Negative	I don't eat **any** cookies.	I don't eat **any** rice.
Question	Do you have **any** cookies?	Do you have **any** rice?
	Do you want **some** cookies?	Do you want **some** rice?
• In questions that are requests or offers, use *some*.		

D Complete the sentences with *some* or *any*.

EXAMPLE: I want ___some___ soup for dinner.

1. My sister wants _____ potatoes.

2. Do you want _____ salad?

3. Lien often eats _____ bread with her lunch.

4. Does she eat _____ sweets?

5. We don't eat _____ pizza.

6. The children want _____ pancakes for breakfast.

7. He doesn't have _____ beef today.

8. The dog doesn't drink _____ milk.

9. Tan is drinking _____ tea with dinner.

10. Do you want _____ coffee?

11. Do you have _____ oranges?

12. We need _____ apples.

E Circle the correct sentence.

EXAMPLE: Silvia needs any bread from the store. / ⟨Silvia needs some bread from the store.⟩

1. She needs some green beans, too. / She needs any green beans, too.

2. She doesn't need some carrots. / She doesn't need any carrots.

3. Augustin wants any rice. / Augustin wants some rice.

4. He doesn't buy any onions. / He doesn't buy some onions.

5. They need some fish for the restaurant. / They need any fish for the restaurant.

6. Augustin buys any beverages every week. / Augustin buys some beverages every week.

7. We don't usually buy any ice cream. / We don't usually buy some ice cream.

8. I don't want some ice cream. / I don't want any ice cream.

9. Do you want some ice cream now? / Do you want any ice cream now?

10. We are buying some cans of soup. / We are buying any cans of soup.

F Write questions about the shopping list in Exercise B based on the answers.

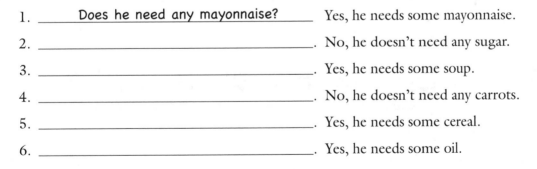

1. ____Does he need any mayonnaise?____ Yes, he needs some mayonnaise.

2. _____. No, he doesn't need any sugar.

3. _____. Yes, he needs some soup.

4. _____. No, he doesn't need any carrots.

5. _____. Yes, he needs some cereal.

6. _____. Yes, he needs some oil.

G Make a shopping list. Ask a partner what you need.

Some/Any

Food and Nutrition

EXTENSION CHALLENGE 2 ➤ *There is / There are*

(A) Read the store directory.

Product	Section	Aisle	Product	Section	Aisle	Product	Section	Aisle
Apples	*Produce*	1	Cheese	*Dairy*	5	Ice cream	*Frozen Foods*	5
Bread	*Bakery*	2	Chicken	*Meats*	8			
Brown sugar	*Baking Needs*	4	Cookies	*Bakery*	2	Lettuce	*Produce*	1
						Milk	*Dairy*	5
Butter	*Dairy*	5	Cream	*Dairy*	5	Oranges	*Produce*	1
Cake	*Bakery*	2	Cucumbers	*Produce*	1	Pears	*Produce*	1
Cake mix	*Baking Needs*	4	Eggs	*Dairy*	5	Soup	*Canned Goods*	3
Canned corn	*Canned Goods*	3	Flour	*Baking Needs*	4			
Canned peas	*Canned Goods*	3	Ground beef	*Meats*	8	Sugar	*Baking Needs*	4
						Turkey	*Meats*	8
Cantaloupe	*Produce*	1	Ham	*Meats*	8	Yogurt	*Dairy*	5

(B) Read the paragraph.

Rando's Market is a great store. For example, they have very fresh fruits and vegetables. There are carrots, for example, that taste like they are fresh from the ground the same day. My favorite produce includes their oranges, apples, corn, potatoes, and lettuce. I also like the meat. It is cut fresh every day. I always shop at Rando's!

(C) Answer the questions about Rando's.

1. What is fresh at Rando's? _____

2. What vegetables do they have? _____

3. What fruit do they have? _____

(D) Read the chart.

There is / There are	
Singular	**There is (There's)** a good Vietnamese restaurant in Portland.
	There is (There's) one bottle of soda for lunch.
Plural	**There are** carrots in Aisle 4.
	There are three pieces of cake.
Questions	**Is there** a dairy section in this supermarket?
	Are there many Chinese restaurants in Los Angeles?
• Use *there* to show or ask about place or position.	

omplete the sentences with *there is* or *there are*.

EXAMPLE: _____There is_____ a new supermarket in Newtown.

1. _____ six aisles in the supermarket.

2. _____ a checkout near the exit.

3. _____ many beverages in aisle two.

4. _____ a good bakery section.

5. _____ tomatoes, potatoes, and carrots in the produce section.

6. _____ cake mixes in aisle three.

7. _____ a section for coffee and tea.

8. _____ canned goods in Aisle five.

9. _____ one aisle for baking goods.

10. _____ three old supermarkets in Newtown.

F Write questions using *is there* and *are there*.

EXAMPLE: a good American restaurant _____Is there a good American restaurant?_____

1. ten tables in the restaurant _____

2. a new cook _____

3. many people in the restaurant today _____

4. six main courses on the menu _____

5. many soups and salads _____

6. a dinner salad on the menu _____

7. hamburgers and cheeseburgers _____

8. many different beverages _____

9. many special desserts _____

10. good chocolate cheesecake _____

G What foods do you find at your local market? Make a list. Then, talk about the food in a group. Use *there is* or *there are*.

_____ _____ _____
_____ _____ _____
_____ _____ _____
_____ _____ _____
_____ _____ _____
_____ _____ _____

Housing

CHALLENGE 1 ➤ Information Questions with *Be* and *Do*

(A) **Read about Ahmed.**

My Housing Experience

I lived in a small house in Oakland, California. I needed more room. I needed something with a bigger yard and four bedrooms. In the summer I found a beautiful house, but the rent was too high, and it was far from my work. The rent was $1,500 a month. I liked it so much that I got a second job to pay the rent. I am happy in my new house, but I have to work a lot, so I am not there very much.

(B) **For each question, circle the letter of the correct answer.**

1. Why did Ahmed need a new house?
   a. He needed a bigger garage for his cars.
   b. His house was too small.
   c. He is happy in his new house.

2. How many bedrooms does the new house have?
   a. The rent is too high.
   b. It has four bedrooms.
   c. The rent is $1,500 a month.

3. Where is the house?
   a. It has a bigger yard.
   b. He found it in the summer.
   c. It is far from his work.

4. How can he afford his house?
   a. It's far from work.
   b. He got a second job.
   c. He works overtime.

(C) **Read the chart.**

Information Questions with *Be* and *Do*			
Information word	***Be***	**Information**	**Example answer**
How much (money)	is	the rent?	$1,500 a month.
	are	the flowers?	$20.00.
Where	is	the apartment?	On First Street.
	are	the apartments?	
What kind of home	is	for rent?	An apartment.
What kinds of homes	are	in the neighborhood?	Apartments and houses.
Information word	***Do* + subject**	**Base verb**	**Example answer**
How much (money)	do you	have?	$20.00.
Where	do you	live?	On First Street.
What kind of home	do you	have?	An apartment.
What kinds of homes	do you		Apartments and houses.
How many bedrooms	does it	have?	Three.

D Complete the questions.

1. How much _____ the cars? ○ is ● are ○ do you have
2. What furniture _____ in your apartment? ○ is ○ are ○ do you
3. Where _____ sleep? ○ is you ○ are you ○ do you
4. How many _____ do you have? ○ car ○ cars ○ money
5. How much _____ need? ○ is you ○ are you ○ do you
6. What kind of cars _____ in the garage? ○ is ○ are ○ do you
7. What kind of sofa _____ need? ○ is you ○ are you ○ do you
8. Where _____ the TV? ○ is ○ are ○ do you

E Match the question with the answer.

1. Where is the chair?
2. How much is the house?
3. Where do you live?
4. What kind of home is on Palm Ave?
5. How many beds do you have?

a. $175,000
b. a condominium
c. in the bedroom
d. seven
e. in Fullerton

F Answer the questions about you.

1. What kind of home do you have? _____
2. Where do you go to school? _____
3. How many brothers and sisters do you have? _____
4. How many bedrooms does your home have? _____

G Answer the questions about your partner.

1. What kind of home do you have? _____
2. Where do you go to school? _____
3. How many brothers and sisters do you have? _____
4. How many bedrooms does your home have? _____

UNIT 4 Housing

CHALLENGE 2 ➤ Information Questions with *which*

A Read the classified ads.

1.
FOR RENT
3 bdrm, 2 bath apt,
utils. pd, $1,025.
Call Angela @ 555-9922.

2.
For Rent
1 bdrm, 1 bath condo, air,
big yard, pets OK, deposit,
$1,400/month, new appliances,
nr. schools and park.
Call Betty, 555-3311.

3.
FOR RENT
1 bath, 1 bd.,
perfect for first home,
air, n/pets, $900,
pool. Sam, 555-3456.

4.
FOR RENT
House – nr. schools, new
appliances, 4 bed, 2 bath,
2 story, big yard. Call 555-7711,
Frank. $1,800/m.

5.
FOR RENT
3 bedroom, 2 bath condo,
nr. park, furnished, fireplace.
Ginger – 555-2311.
$1,200.

6.
FOR RENT
2 bd, 2 bth mobile home
near school, new carpet,
good neighborhood.
$1,200 rent. Call 555-9912.

B Complete the chart about the classified ads.

Kind of home	Number of bedrooms	Number of bathrooms	Rental price	Phone number
1. apartment	3	2	$1,025	555-9922
2.				
3.				
4.				
5.				
6.				

C Read the chart.

Information Questions with *which*				
Information word	**Subject**	**Verb**	**Information**	**Example question**
which	house	has	three bedrooms	**Which** house has three bedrooms?
	houses	have	a pool	**Which** houses have three bedrooms?
			a fireplace	
			a big yard	
	house	is	on First Street	**Which** house is on First Street?
	houses	are	next to the park	**Which** houses are on First Street?
				Which houses are next to the park?

Use the words to write questions.

1. house / is / near my school / which _____ Which house is near my school? _____

2. have / houses / which / two bathrooms _____

3. which / has / house / a balcony _____

4. houses / are / which / big _____

5. has / apartment / which / furniture _____

6. is / condo / which / expensive _____

7. car / which / in the garage / is _____

8. at 10:00 A.M. which / starts / class _____

E **Answer the questions about the classified ads in Exercise A.**

1. Which homes have two bathrooms? _____ Ads 1, 4, 5, and 6 include two bathrooms. _____

2. Which homes are condominiums? _____

3. Which home has a pool? _____

4. Which homes are cheap? _____

5. Which home is the most expensive? _____

6. Which two-bedroom home is $1,200? _____

F **Read the classified ads. Write questions with *which*. Use Exercise E as a model.**

1. **For Rent**
1 bed, 1 bath, view, fireplace, pool, house near schools, a/c. Call 555-5672.

2. **FOR RENT**
2 bed, 2 bath, apt, util paid, gd neighborhood, nr schools. Call Frank 555-0923.

3. **FOR RENT**
5 bed, 3 bath hse, view, pool, 2-car garage, landscaping. Mollie 555-9898.

1. _____

2. _____

3. _____

4. _____

5. _____

6. _____

Housing

CHALLENGE 3 ➤ Information Questions

A Complete a rental application with the information from the box.

Javier	2 years 6 months	Santa Clara	(408) 555-2234	94801
97235 Artesia Place	CA	Mechanic	Anchor Motors	

RENTAL APPLICATION

Name: _Aguilar_ _____
last   first   mi

Present Address: _334 W. Horton Blvd._

City: _____ State: _CA_ Zip: _95050_

Prior Address: _____

City: _Richmond_ _____ State: _____ Zip: _____

Employer: _____

Position: _____

Phone: ( )

Work Phone: _(408) 555-7698_

How long? _____
years/months

Phone: _(408) 555-2543_

How long? _8 years 3 months_
years/months

B Read the chart.

Information Question	Example answer
What is your name?	My name is Javier Aguilar.
Where do you live now?	I live in Santa Clara.
Where did you live before?	I lived in Richmond.
How long did you live there?	I lived there three years.
Who is your employer?	I work for Anchor Motors.
What is your position?	I am a mechanic.

Information Questions

C. Write questions based on the answers below.

1. My last name is Johnson. <u>What is your last name?</u>

2. My bank is Americana Bank. <u>What</u>

3. I go to school in Santa Clara. <u>Where</u>

4. I worked in Santa Clara for three years. <u>How long</u>

5. My supervisor is John Carpenter. <u>Who</u>

6. I lived in Monterey. <u>Where</u>

D. Match each question to an answer.

1. Where did you study English?   a. Steve Hampson

2. How long did you study English?   b. 9976 W. Broadway

3. Who was your teacher?   c. at Palm City Adult School

4. What is the address?   d. four years

E. Write a conversation with the questions and answers in Exercise D. Then, practice with a partner.

Student A: <u>Where did you study English?</u>

Student B: _____

Student A: _____

Student B: _____

Student A: _____

Student B: _____

Student A: _____

Student B: _____

F. Ask a partner questions about Exercise A.

EXAMPLE: *Student A:* What's his name?
　　　　　　Student B: It's Javier Aguilar.

CHALLENGE 4 ➤ Prepositions of Location

A List the furniture and other items in the picture of the kitchen above.

●	clock

B Read the chart.

Prepositions			
The ball is **in** the box.		The ball is **between** two boxes.	
The ball is **on** the box.		The ball is **over** the box.	
The ball is **under** the box.		The ball is **in front of** the box.	
The ball is **next to** the box.		The ball is **behind** the box.	

- Use prepositions to talk about where things are.

C Circle the correct prepositions in each sentence.

EXAMPLE: There are six rooms (in) / on my apartment.

1. The kitchen is **on / next to** the living room.
2. The microwave is **between / over** the stove.
3. The washer is **on / in** the kitchen.
4. The refrigerator is **next to / under** the stove.
5. The apples are **in back of / in** the refrigerator.
6. The butter is **next to / in** the apples.

7. The sofa is **between / on** two windows.
8. The flowers are **in / on** the coffee table.
9. The book is **under / in** the armchair.
10. The TV is **under / in front of** the armchair.
11. The vacuum cleaner is **in / in back of** the sofa.
12. The door is **between / over** the sofa and the chair.

D Use the words to write sentences.

EXAMPLE:
in / is / the house / a quiet neighborhood

The house is in a quiet neighborhood.

1. Madison Street / the house / is / on _____
2. behind / the swimming pool / is / the house _____
3. the yard / of / is / in / the house / front _____
4. are / the corner / the flowers / in _____
5. is / the garage / next / the house / to _____
6. over / the balcony / is / the door _____
7. in / is / the fireplace / the living room _____
8. between / the bathroom / is / two bedrooms _____
9. is / under / the dishwasher / the kitchen counter _____
10. over / the kitchen counter / the cupboard / is _____

E Make a list of furniture and other things in the classroom.

1. _____clock_____   3. _____   5. _____
2. _____   4. _____   6. _____

F Write sentences about the locations of things in your list in Exercise E.

1. The clock is on the wall. _____
2. _____
3. _____
4. _____
5. _____
6. _____

Housing

CHALLENGE 5 ➤ Modals: *May* and *Might*

A Read the budget.

Alan's Budget		
MONTHLY INCOME: $5,467	**Budget Expenses**	**Actual Expenses**
Rent	$1,400	$1,400
Gas ✓	$50	$44
Electric	$140	$165
Water	$35	$31
Food	$1,000	$945
Life insurance	$105	$105
Gasoline	$250	$262
Phone	$175	$145
Entertainment	$400	$462
Clothing	$100	$76
Household repairs	$100	$24
Furniture	$100	$0
Savings	$1,000	$786
Other	$462	$872
TOTAL	**$5,317.00**	**$5,317.00**

B Circle the items that are over budget. Check the items that are under budget.

C Read the chart.

Modals: *May* and *Might* to Show Probability (Use Interchangeably)			
Subject	**Modal**	**Base verb**	**Example sentence**
I, you, he, she, it, we, they	may might	spend earn be	I **may** spend $250 on gasoline this month. You **may** spend $175 on the phone bill. He **may** earn $6,000. Food **might** be $1,000. We **may** earn $3,500 a month. They **may** spend $300 a month on food.

D Rewrite the sentences with *may* to show probability.

1. We move in two weeks. <u>We may move in two weeks.</u>

2. They have a three bedroom house. _____

3. She lives in an apartment on Main Street. _____

4. You need a new job. _____

5. It is a beautiful house. _____

6. He spends $300 a month. _____

E Rewrite the sentences with *might* to show probability.

1. Gasoline is $250. <u>Gasoline might be $250.</u>

2. They need money for clothes. _____

3. She wants help with the rent. _____

4. He earns $6,500 a month. _____

5. We spend $800 on food. _____

6. I go to the bank today. _____

F Complete the sentences about the budget in Exercise A.

1. He may spend $ _____50_____ on gasoline.

2. He might spend $ _____ on furniture.

3. He might earn $ _____ .

4. He may spend $ _____ on the phone bill.

5. He might spend $ _____ on entertainment.

6. He may spend $ _____ on clothing.

G Plan a new budget with a partner. Use *may* and *might*.

MONTHLY EXPENSES		

Housing

EXTENSION CHALLENGE 1 ➤ Combining Sentences with *and*

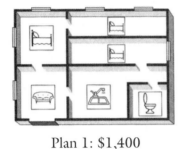

Plan 1: $1,400

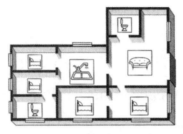

Plan 2: $2,000 NEW

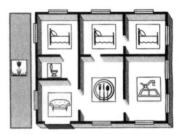

Plan 3: $1,400

A Complete the sentences using the information above.

1. Plan two _____has_____ four _____bedrooms_____. It's _____$2,000_____ a month.

2. Plan three _____ three _____. It is _____ a month.

3. Plans one and three _____have one_____ bathroom. These are _____$1,400_____ a month.

4. Plan two _____ two _____. It also _____ a kitchen on this floor.

B Read the charts.

Combining Sentences with *and*			
Subject		**Subject**	
The house	is in a quiet neighborhood.	**The house**	has a swimming pool.
The house	is in a quiet neighborhood, **and** **it**		has a swimming pool.
The house is in a quiet neighborhood, **and it** has a swimming pool.			

Combining Sentences with *and*			
Subject		**Subject**	
The rooms	have air-conditioning.	**The rooms**	are in good condition.
The rooms	have air-conditioning, **and** **they**		are in good condition.
The rooms have air-conditioning, **and they** are in good condition.			

C Underline the two parts of each sentence and add a comma.

EXAMPLE:
<u>My apartment has five rooms</u>, and <u>it has a beautiful view from the balcony</u>.

1. The rent is $800 a month and the utilities are included.

2. The living room has a fireplace and the kitchen is large.

3. Nikolai and Andrea need an apartment and they are looking in the classified ads.

4. His wife wants an apartment with three bedrooms and she needs a washer/dryer.

5. Our dream house is in a friendly neighborhood and it has a swimming pool.

6. Peter and I are buying a house in September and we need new furniture.

D Combine the two sentences using *and*.

EXAMPLE: I have a new friend. Kyung's name is Kyung Kim.
<u>**I have a new friend, and his name is Kyung Kim.**</u>

1. Kyung moved here from Korea last month. Kyung lives in Arcadia, Florida.

_____

2. The teller (female) is opening a checking account for him. The teller is also opening a savings account.

_____

3. Kyung can get his checks immediately. Kyung can write checks from the checking account.

_____

4. Kyung uses checks to pay for food. Kyung writes the checks in the check ledger.

_____

5. Nam-young Kim writes the check for the rent. She also pays for the utilities.

_____

6. Mr. and Mrs. Kim buy clothes from Sal's Clothes. Mr. and Mrs. Kim buy food from Renco Market.

_____

7. Mr. and Mrs. Kim pay $850 a month for rent. They need $400 a month for food.

_____

8. Their house has three bedrooms. It is in a quiet neighborhood.

_____

E Write two sentences about your home. Then, combine the sentences using *and*.

Sentence 1: _____

Sentence 2: _____

Combined sentence: _____

Housing

EXTENSION CHALLENGE 2 ➤ Adjectives and Noun Modifiers

Adjectives and Noun Modifiers

1.

3.

2.

4.

A Look at the houses. Answer the information questions.

1. Which house is the biggest? _____ Number 2 is the biggest. _____

2. Which house is the smallest? _____

3. Which houses have chimneys? _____

4. Which houses are two-stories? _____

B Read the chart.

Adjectives and Noun Modifiers	
Adjectives	**Noun modifiers**

Adjectives describe nouns.
   I live in a **friendly** neighborhood.
	A noun can sometimes describe another noun.
	   I need a **coffee** table.

Adjectives come before nouns.
   He likes the **big** yard.
	The second noun is more general than the first.
	   A **coffee** table is usually small.

Adjectives do not change for plural nouns.
   You're buying some **new** tables.
	The first noun is always singular.
	   Where are the **coffee** tables?

You can put two adjectives before a noun. Use a comma between the adjectives.
   We want a **large, old** house.
	You can put a number before a noun modifier. Use a hyphen between the number and the modifier.
	   You want a **two-bedroom** apartment.
	   (Meaning: two bedrooms, not two apartments)

C Rewrite the sentences using the adjectives in parentheses.

EXAMPLE: I need a VCR. (new) _____ I need a new VCR. _____

1. The house has a garage. (separate) _____

2. He's buying some flowers. (expensive) _____

3. The balcony has a view. (beautiful) _____

4. These are chairs. (comfortable) _____

5. I live in a neighborhood. (nice / quiet) _____

6. The rent for the apartment is $750. (remodeled) _____

7. We need a dishwasher. (good / cheap) _____

8. What is your address? (prior) _____

9. She wants to rent a house. (big) _____

10. You want some lamps. (small) _____

D Complete each sentence using the nouns given. Put them in the correct order.

EXAMPLE: (ledger / check) I'm looking for my _____ check ledger. _____

1. (account / bank) Are you opening a _____?

2. (ATM / card) I need my _____.

3. (ID / photo) Do you have your _____?

4. (application / forms) Kenji needs to fill out the _____.

5. (house / three / story) He's renting a _____.

6. (dream / house) We are going to buy our _____.

7. (two / car / garage) She wants a _____.

8. (tables / coffee) Where do you want the _____?

E Describe your school and your classroom. Write two sentences with noun modifiers and two with adjectives.

Noun modifiers

_____

_____

Adjectives

_____

_____

Our Community

CHALLENGE 1 ➤ *When, Where, and Prepositions*

A Read the train schedule.

Train Number	560	570	600	625
San Carlos	7:50A	9:50A	12:50P	2:20P
Palm City	8:02A	10:02A	1:02P	2:32P
Franklin City	8:19A	10:19A	1:19P	2:49P
Lakeview	8:34A	10:34A	1:34P	3:04P
Jackson	8:44A	10:44A	1:44P	3:14P
1. Main St	8:49A	10:49A	1:49P	3:19P
2. Broadway	8:54A	10:54A	1:54P	3:24P
3. N. Hart	9:00A	11:00A	2:00P	3:30P
Pleasantville	9:24A	11:24A	2:24P	3:54P
Casper	10:01A	12:01P	3:01P	4:31P

B Answer the questions about the train schedule.

1. How long is the trip from Palm City to Lakeview? _____ 32 minutes _____

2. How long is the trip from Pleasantville to Casper? _____

3. How long is the trip from San Carlos to Casper? _____

4. You want to arrive in Casper in the morning. Which train do you take? _____

5. You want to arrive in Casper around 3:00 P.M. Which train do you take? _____

6. You want to arrive in Casper after 4:30 P.M. What train do you take? _____

C Read the chart.

When, Where, and Prepositions			
	Base verb	Preposition	Example question
When does the bus	stop	**at** (street) **in** (a city)	When does the bus stop **at** Main Street? When does the bus stop **in** Casper?
	leave	∅ (no preposition) **for** (destination) **from** (start)	When does the bus leave Main Street? When does the bus leave **for** Casper? When does the bus leave **for** San Carlos?
	arrive	**from** (start) **at** (street) **in** (city)	When does the bus arrive **from** San Carlos? When does it arrive **at** Main Street? When does it arrive **in** Casper?
Where does the bus	stop	**in** (city)	Where does the bus stop **in** Jackson?

D Circle the correct preposition.

1. When does the train stop **in** / **on** San Carlos?
2. Where does the bus stop **in** / **on** Pleasantville?
3. When does the train arrive **in** / **at** North Hart Street?
4. When does the bus leave **for** / **∅** Pleasantville?
5. Where does the train stop **for** / **in** San Carlos?
6. Where does the train stop **for** / **in** Richmond?
7. When does the bus arrive **from** / **∅** Los Angeles?
8. When does the train leave **for** / **∅** Broadway?

E Look at the schedule in Exercise A. Complete the sentences.

1. Train 600 arrives in _____Lakeview_____ at 1:34 P.M.
2. Train 570 leaves for _____ from Palm City at _____.
3. Train 625 stops in _____ at _____ at 3:24 P.M.
4. Train 570 arrives from _____ at 10:44 A.M.
5. Train 560 leaves _____ at 9:24 A.M.
6. Train 625 stops at _____ in _____ at 3:24 P.M.

F Ask a partner questions about the train schedule in Exercise A. Use *when* and *where*.

G Create a possible train schedule for your area.

Train Number	560	570	600	625

H Ask a partner about his or her bus schedule. Use *when* or *where*.

UNIT 5 Our Community

CHALLENGE 2 ➤ Simple Present

A Look at the directory.

COMMUNITY DIRECTORY

City Hall..555-7834
1285 W. Harbor Blvd.

Courthouse..555-7845
1287 W. Harbor Blvd.

DMV *(Department of Motor Vehicles)*
Information.......................................555-7777
Appointments 555-7778
92 W. Archer Blvd.

Schools *(Public)*
Alton Junior High...........................555-2964
34 Alton Parkway
Lincoln High...................................555-8336
278 Lincoln Ave
Washington Elementary..................555-5437
210 Washington St.

Fire Department................................555-8461
Emergencies call 911
687 Broadway Ave.

Police Department.............................555-7820
Emergencies call 911
1200 W. Harbor Blvd.

Playgrounds and Parks
Department of Parks
and Recreation.................................555-8612
1295 Harbor Blvd.
Carlton Park
11278 Park Lane
Keaton Park
2 Ridge Route

Library *(Public)*.................................555-1236
22 S. Banning Ave.

U. S. Post Office.................................555-6245
151 E. Broadway

B Complete the chart with information from the directory in Exercise A.

Need or Problem	Agency Name	Phone Number
I need a driver's license.	DMV	555-777 / 555-7778
I need to register for high school.		
A house is on fire.		

C Read the chart.

Simple Present		
Subject	**Verb**	**Example sentence**
I, you, we, they	want	I **want** a new car.
	need	You **need** the number to the hospital.
	call	We **call** for assistance.
	look (for)	They **look** for information in the directory.
he, she	wants	He **wants** to mail a package.
	needs	She **needs** a driver's license.
	calls	He **calls** the courthouse every week.
	looks (for)	She **looks** for books.

D **Complete each sentence with the correct form of the verb in the simple present.**

1. Kenji _____ needs _____ (need) the police immediately.

2. The women _____ (call) the hospital every hour.

3. He _____ (want) to mail a package to his mother in Columbia.

4. She _____ (look) for places to have a picnic in the city directory.

5. We _____ (call) the DMV when we buy a new car.

6. I _____ (like) the doctor on Main Street.

7. She _____ (prefer) to go to a park.

8. The nurse _____ (call) the doctor every day.

9. We _____ (eat) lunch at the restaurant on the corner.

10. The bus _____ (stop) on the corner of Main and Nutwood.

11. I _____ (visit) Marie on Saturdays.

12. My husband _____ (come) with me to the hospital.

E **Write reasons why Raquel may call. What do you think?**

1. (bank) Raquel needs money. _____

2. (dentist) Raquel _____

3. (shoe store) Raquel _____

4. (doctors) Raquel and Mario _____

5. (optometrist) Raquel _____

6. (hospital) Raquel and Mario _____

7. (DMV) Raquel _____

8. (fire department) Mario _____

F **Write reasons you might call a restaurant, a bank, and a rental car agency.**

1. (restaurant) _____

2. (bank) _____

3. (rental car agency) _____

Our Community

CHALLENGE 3 ➤ Imperatives

Imperatives

A Look at the map.

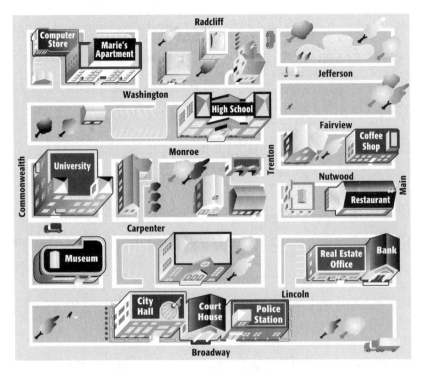

B Follow the directions and identify the location.

1. Start at the corner of Broadway and Main. Go north on Main Street. Turn left on Nutwood. Turn right on Trenton. Stop on the right. What is on the corner of Washington?
   _____the high school_____

2. Start at the corner of Commonwealth and Broadway. Go east on Broadway. Stop on the left. What is before the Court House? _____

3. Start at the corner of Commonwealth and Radcliff. Go south on Commonwealth. Turn left on Washington. What is on the left before the high school? _____

C Read the chart.

Imperatives			
	(Negative) Verb	**Information**	**Example sentence**
~~you~~	**(don't) go**	straight straight ahead	**Go** straight three blocks. **Don't go** straight ahead.
	(don't) turn	left right around	**Turn** left on Nutwood. **Don't turn** right on Nutwood. **Turn** around.
	(don't) stop	on the left on the right	**Stop** on the left. **Don't stop** on the right.

D) Underline the imperatives in the following paragraph. The first one is done for you.

Here are the directions to get to my new apartment from the bank. <u>Go</u> north on Emerson Street. Walk straight ahead for two blocks. There is a pharmacy on the left. Turn left on Michigan Avenue. Go two blocks. At the intersection of Michigan Avenue and Lincoln Street, turn right. Don't turn left; that's the way to my old apartment. My new apartment is at the end of Lincoln Street, on the left. Walk up the stairs. Find apartment #3.

E) Make the affirmative sentence negative.

1. Go to the post office today. <u>Don't go to the post office today.</u>

2. Write your address on the form. _____

3. Fill in all the customer forms now. _____

4. Walk from the post office to the pharmacy. _____

5. Turn right at the next intersection. _____

6. Stop at the corner of Main and Robinson. _____

F) Make the negative sentences affirmative.

1. Don't send the package economy class. <u>Send the package economy class.</u>

2. Don't buy insurance for the package. _____

3. Don't turn left at the corner. _____

4. Don't go west on Broadway. _____

G) Give directions using the map in Exercise A.

1. You are at the corner of Commonwealth and Radcliff. Give directions to the university.

_____

_____

2. You are at the corner of Main and Jefferson. Give directions to the museum.

_____

_____

3. You are at the intersection of Trenton and Lincoln. Give directions to the courthouse.

_____

_____

Imperatives

UNIT 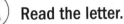 5

Our Community

CHALLENGE 4 ➤ Simple Present and Present Continuous

 A Read the letter.

> Dear Claudia,
>   Hello! How are you doing? I am studying English here in Palm City with Marie. She is a good friend. We go to school every day. She also works Monday through Friday at the hospital. Sometimes we have lunch at a park near the hospital. I am studying right now. My English is improving. I often walk to the post office in the mornings. I hope to receive a letter from you.
>   I am very happy here, but I miss Antonio. I am working hard on English so I can go home soon. I hope to see you soon before I go home. Please write.
> Your friend,
> Raquel

B Answer the questions about the letter.

1. Why does Raquel go to the post office?

   a. The post office is near the apartment.

   b. She wants to get a letter from her friend.

   c. She goes in the morning.

2. Why is Raquel going home soon?

   a. She wants to see her friend.

   b. She is happy.

   c. She wants to see Antonio.

C Read the charts.

Simple Present					
Subject	Verb	Subject	Verb	
I, you, we, they	eat	I	am	happy
		you, we, they	are	sad
he, she	eats	he, she, it	is	tired

Present Continuous			
Subject	Be	Base+*ing*	Example sentence
I	am	writing	I **am writing** this letter in English.
you, we, they	are	going	We **are going** to the mall.
he, she	is	eating	He **is eating** at the coffee shop.

- Use simple present with *always, often, usually, never, sometimes,* and *every day*.
- Use the present continuous with *right now, at this moment,* and *today*.

D **Complete each sentence with the simple present or the present continuous.**

EXAMPLE: You never _____ to the hardware store. ○ are going ● go

1. Marie _____ a new job at the hospital. ○ is having ○ has
2. Today she _____ in the morning. ○ is working ○ works
3. Michel sometimes _____ Marie. ○ visits ○ is visiting
4. They always _____ to the museum. ○ are going ○ go
5. I _____ in a condominium at the moment. ○ live ○ am living
6. My husband and I _____ to the supermarket every day. ○ are going ○ go
7. You usually _____ lunch at Taco Town. ○ have ○ are having
8. Right now you _____ in the park. ○ are eating ○ eat

E **Complete each sentence with the correct form of the simple present or the present continuous.**

EXAMPLE: I _____ am going _____ (go) to the dentist today.

1. I often _____ (walk) to the dentist.
2. Today I _____ (take) the bus.
3. My sister usually _____ (go) with me.
4. At the moment, we _____ (wait) at the bus stop on Main Street.
5. The bus always _____ (stop) at the corner of Main and Washington.
6. Anya and Ivan often _____ (take) the bus, too.
7. They _____ (go) to the travel agency right now.
8. Every summer, they _____ (visit) their family in Russia.
9. You sometimes _____ (wait) for the bus at the stop on High Street.
10. At the moment, you _____ (read) the newspaper at the bus stop.

F **Complete the letter.**

Dear _____,

How are you? I am fine. At this moment, I _____(go) to school in

_____ (city). My school's name _____ (be)_____.

Right now I _____ (study) English. My class starts at _____. I always

_____ (work) hard. My teacher _____ (be) very friendly. Right now,

we _____ (learn) about _____.

Your friend,

_____

Our Community

CHALLENGE 5 ➤ Simple Past

Simple Past

Jennifer Gault
_____
_____

_____
_____
_____
_____

A Complete the envelope with the information below.

To:

8246 Wilson St.	97701
John Gil	Bend, OR

From:

33010	Miami, FL
Jennifer Gault	895 Main Place

B Read the charts.

Simple Past (Regular)		
Subject	**Verb (base+*ed*)**	**Example sentence**
I, you, he, she, it, we, they	talked	I **talked** with Marie.
	wanted	She **wanted** a sandwich.
	walked	We **walked** in the park.

Simple Past (Irregular)		
Subject	**Verb**	**Example sentence**
I, you, he, she, it, we, they	went (go)	I **went** to the park.
	ate (eat)	She **ate** at the coffee shop.
	bought (buy)	We **bought** new dresses.
	sent (send)	They **sent** a letter.

C Complete the sentences with the simple past.

1. She _____wanted_____ (want) a new job.

2. Raquel and Marie _____ (buy) lunch at Taco Town.

3. You _____ (go) to school every day.

4. We _____ (walk) to the post office for the mail.

5. I _____ (eat) with my friend.

6. She _____ (talk) to the doctor about her husband.

D Complete the letter with the simple past form of the verbs.

Dear Kenji,

How are you? I am now here in Palm City. I _____went_____ (go) to school yesterday.
The teacher _____ (talk) to me about my goals. I want a new job. Last year,
I only _____ (want) help with my English. Now I am studying more. My teacher
is very good.

I _____(talk) to Beverly. We _____ (talk) about our goals. She
wants to go to a university. We _____ (go) to a restaurant. I _____
(eat) sushi. I like sushi. I _____ (send) a letter to Beverly after lunch.

E Answer the questions with complete sentences.

1. What did you eat last night for dinner?

   _____

2. What did a classmate eat last night?

   _____

3. Who did you talk to after class last week?

   _____

4. Who did a classmate talk to after class last week?

   _____

5. Where did you go last week after class?

   _____

6. Where did a classmate go last week after class?

   _____

Our Community

EXTENSION CHALLENGE 1 ➤ Prepositions of Location

A Read the map.

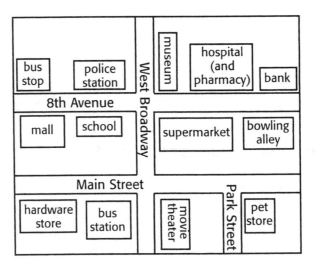

B Write the places in the community in the chart. Use the map above.

Service	Buy and Sell
police station	

C Read the chart.

Prepositions of Location	
Preposition	**Example**
in	There is a hospital **in** Thomasville.
on	It is **on** Main Street.
at	It is **at** the intersection of Main Street and Northern Avenue.
near	It is **near** my house.
between	My house is **between** South Street and Washington Street.
next to	It is **next to** the police station.
on the corner (of)	The police station is **on the corner of** South Street and Pine Street.
across from	It is **across from** the post office.
on the right	The courthouse is **on the right**.
on the left	The fire station is **on the left**.

D Look at the map of Newtown. Write *yes* or *no* for each statement.

EXAMPLE: The bank is next to the fire station. __yes__

1. The pet store is next to the coffee shop. _____

2. The bank is at the corner of Main and High. _____

3. The fire station is across from the police station. _____

4. The park is near the library. _____

5. The hospital is on the corner of High Street. _____

6. There is a courthouse in Newtown. _____

7. The library is on High Street. _____

8. The coffee shop is between the pet store and the gas station. _____

9. You are on High Street. Turn right on Main Street. The park is on the left. _____

10. You are on High Street. Turn left on Main Street. The hospital is on the right. _____

Newtown

E Using the map in Exercise A, complete each sentence with the name of a place.

EXAMPLE: The school is near _____the mall_____.

1. The movie theater is on _____.

2. The bus stop is at the end of _____.

3. The bowling alley is next to _____.

4. The hardware store is near _____.

5. The hospital is between _____ and _____.

6. The pharmacy is in _____.

7. The police station is across from _____.

8. The pet store is on the corner of _____ and _____.

F List three places in your community.

1. _____ 2. _____ 3. _____

G Describe the location of the three places in Exercise F. Use complete sentences and prepositions of location.

1. _____

2. _____

3. _____

EXTENSION CHALLENGE 2 ➤ Prch text of Time

Prepositions of Time

A Read the calendar.

SEPTEMBER 2009						
Sunday	**Monday**	**Tuesday**	**Wednesday**	**Thursday**	**Friday**	**Saturday**
		1	2 Doctor's Appt. 2 P.M.	3	4 Meeting with Marjorie 1 P.M.	5
6	7	8 library P.M.	9 library P.M.	10 library P.M.	11	12
13	14 Fly to NY 7 A.M.	15	16	17	18	19
20	21	22	23	24 Dentist Appt. 4 P.M.	25	26
27	28	29	30			

B Complete the chart about Oneida's schedule.

Event	Date	Time
doctor's appt.	9/2/2009	2 P.M.

C Read the chart.

Prepositions of Time		
Preposition	**Information**	**Example sentence**
on	days	I am going to the bank **on** Saturday.
	dates	City Hall is not open **on** July 4.
at	a specific time	I am going to the dentist **at** 3:00 P.M.
	night	We go to the library **at** night.
in	amount of time	He's going to Japan **in** two hours.
	months	He always visits his sister **in** August.
	seasons	The weather is very warm **in** the summer.
	the morning / afternoon / evening	We go to the bowling alley **in** the afternoon.

D Circle the correct preposition for each sentence.

EXAMPLE: Stefan always visits Kenji **at** / **(in)** the summer.

1. He usually comes **in** / **on** August.

2. This year, he is coming **in** / **on** July 14.

3. His bus arrives **at** / **in** 10:00 A.M.

4. It arrives **in** / **at** night.

5. Kenji and Stefan are going to the museum **in** / **on** Sunday.

6. They're going **in** / **at** the afternoon.

7. They're going to the theater **in** / **at** the evening.

8. The show is **at** / **on** 8:30 P.M.

9. **In** / **On** two hours, they're going to the mall.

10. Stefan is going home **on** / **at** July 20.

11. Kenji wants to visit Stefan **in** / **at** May.

12. He likes to travel **in** / **on** the spring.

E Complete each sentence with the correct preposition.

EXAMPLE: Palm City is a wonderful place to visit __in__ the summer.

1. The temperature is usually 80 degrees Fahrenheit _____ the afternoon.

2. _____ night, it is often about 70 degrees.

3. It was 85 degrees _____ July 30.

4. People in Palm City sometimes eat their lunch in the park _____ 12:00 P.M.

5. They also like to walk in the park _____ the evening.

6. The children always play in the playgrounds _____ June, July, and August.

7. You usually see them in the playgrounds _____ Friday and Saturday.

8. Palm City is also a nice place to visit _____ the winter.

9. Most of the time, the weather is warm _____ January.

10. The temperature is usually about 65 degrees _____ 8:00 A.M.

F Look at the calendar in Exercise A. Answer the questions in complete sentences.

1. When is Oneida going to New York?

   She is going to New York on September 14 at 7:00 A.M.

2. When does she have a meeting with Marjorie?

   _____

3. When does Marjorie go to the library?

   _____

4. It is now 2 P.M. on September 24. When will Marjorie go to the dentist?

   _____

UNIT 6 **Health**

CHALLENGE 1 ➤ Using *Need to*

A Read about the everyday habits.

Kenji

Gilberto

Lien

Sleep: 7 hours
Exercise: 10 minutes
Eat: 2 meals

Sleep: 8 hours
Exercise: 30 minutes
Eat: 3 meals

Sleep: 9 hours
Exercise: 0 minutes
Eat: 3 meals

B Rank the students in Exercise A. Number 1 has the best habits. Write the names.

1. _____Gilberto_____

2. _____

3. _____

C Read the chart.

Verb + Infinitive			
Subject	**Verb**	**Infinitive (*to* + base)**	**Example sentence**
I, you, we, they	want	sleep	I **want to sleep** eight hours.
	need	relax	You **need to relax** after work.
	like	work	We **like to work** in the morning.
he, she	wants	to { drink	They **want to drink** a lot of water.
	needs	eat	He **likes to eat** a snack in the afternoon.
	likes	exercise	She **likes to exercise** regularly.

D Circle the correct word or words.

1. Kim (likes to) / likes eat pizza for lunch.
2. Larry and Jean want / want to good food for dinner.
3. We need / need to exercise every day.
4. I like / like to walk in the morning.
5. Kenji likes to / likes pizza for lunch.
6. We work to / work on Saturday.
7. You need / need to drink a lot of water.
8. They relax to / relax after dinner.

E Complete the sentences.

1. Edgar _____wants to_____ (want) work on Saturday.
2. Natalie _____ (need) exercise more.
3. Karen and Grace _____ (eat) three meals a day.
4. Kenji _____ (exercise) ten minutes a day.
5. Paul and Claudia _____ (want) shoes for work.
6. Tien and Huong _____ (drink) water for dinner.
7. Gilberto _____ (need) sleep more.
8. Cathy _____ (like) relax at night.

F Complete the chart about what you and a partner want to do.

I want . . .	My partner wants . . .
_____	_____
_____	_____
_____	_____
_____	_____

We both want . . .
_____
_____
_____
_____

UNIT **6**

Health

CHALLENGE 2 ➤ Comparative and Superlative Adjectives

 A What ailments do you have more? Number the ailments 1–8. Number 1 is the ailment you have most.

_____ a backache

_____ a cold

_____ a headache

_____ a runny nose

_____ a sore throat

_____ a stomachache

_____ a toothache

_____ the flu

 B Talk to a partner. Compare your partner's answers to yours in Exercise A.

C Read the charts.

Adjective	Comparative Adjective	Superlative Adjective
serious	more serious	the most serious
	less serious	the least serious
common	more common	the most common
	less common	the least common

Comparatives	Superlatives
The flu is **more serious** *than* a cold.	Sometimes a toothache is the **most serious** ailment, and a cold is the **least serious**.
A stomachache is **less serious** *than* a toothache.	
A headache is **more common** *than* the flu.	Maybe a cold is the **most common** ailment, and a toothache is the **least common**.
A toothache is **less common** *than* a cold.	

D **Use the words to make sentences. Sometimes there can be more than one answer.**

1. is / serious / a cold / than / more / a runny nose
   A cold is more serious than a runny nose.

2. the most / a sore throat / serious / is / ailment
   _____

3. common / is / the / than / flu / more / toothache / a
   _____

4. less / serious / a backache / than / a runny nose / is
   _____

5. the / common / most / ailment / is / a bad headache
   _____

6. serious / less / a cold / is / than / a backache
   _____

7. less / common / a cold / the flu / than / is
   _____

8. serious / most / the / the flu / is / ailment
   _____

E **Answer the questions about the ailments in Exercise A with complete sentences.**

1. What is more serious, the flu or a cold?
   The flu is more serious than a cold.

2. What is most serious, a sore throat, a runny nose, or a cold?
   _____

3. What is more common, a backache or a toothache?
   _____

4. What is less serious, a headache or a cold?
   _____

5. What is less common, a sore throat or a headache?
   _____

6. What is most common, a cold, the flu, or a backache?
   _____

F **What do you think is the most serious and the most common ailment? Write sentences.**

1. (most serious) _____
2. (most common) _____
3. (least serious) _____
4. (least common) _____

Comparative and Superlative Adjectives

UNIT 6 Health

CHALLENGE 3 ➤ Simple Past: Regular and Irregular

A Match the phrases to make sentences.

1. Anya talked   a. in the park every week.

2. She exercised   b. cigarettes.

3. She walked   c. to a doctor.

4. She also smoked   d. three times a week.

B Write the sentences in Exercise A into a paragraph.

> Anya talked to a doctor.

C Read the charts.

Regular Simple Past	
Subject	**Verb (base + *ed*)**
I, you, he, she, we, they	walked (walk)
	talked (talk)
	smoked (smoke)
	played (play)

Irregular Simple Past	
Subject	**Verb**
I, you, he, she, we, they	had (have)
	went (go)
	said (say)

Irregular Simple Past: *Be*		
Subject	**Be verb**	**Example sentence**
I, he, she	was	I **was** sick.
you, we, they	were	You **were** at the hospital.

D Circle the correct verb form.

EXAMPLE: Last year, Luc **has** / **(had)** some health problems.

1. He **was** / **were** in the hospital a lot.
2. His wife **be** / **was** very nervous.
3. I **were** / **was** very healthy last year.
4. I **had** / **having** a good exercise plan.
5. You **were** / **was** sick last week.

6. You **had** / **having** a headache.
7. My wife and I **has** / **had** a bad day yesterday.
8. We **was** / **were** both very tired.
9. My dog **had** / **have** a broken leg last year.
10. The children **was** / **were** very sad about it.

E Complete the sentences with the simple past tense of the verb.

1. Last week, Alex _____exercised_____ (exercise) every day.
2. He also _____ (play) tennis on Saturday.
3. He _____ (want) his wife to play tennis, too.
4. On Saturday, she _____ (visit) the doctor.
5. She _____ (ask) for medicine for more energy.
6. She _____ (need) more exercise and not medicine.
7. She also _____ (smoke) a pack of cigarettes a day.
8. She _____ (talk) to her husband about it.

F Write the sentences in Exercise E in a paragraph.

Last week, Alex exercised every day.

Health

CHALLENGE 4 ➤ Modal: *Should*

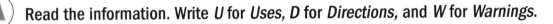

A Read the information. Write *U* for *Uses*, *D* for *Directions*, and *W* for *Warnings*.

1. __D__ Take 1 or 2 tablets with water every 4 hours while symptoms persist.

2. __U__ For temporary relief of sore throat pain.

3. _____ Spray four times into throat.

4. _____ For external use only.

5. _____ For temporary relief of cold and flu symptoms.

6. __W__ Do not drive a motor vehicle while taking this medication.

7. _____ To help prevent infection in minor cuts and scrapes.

8. _____ Children with the flu or chicken pox should NOT take this medication.

9. _____ Take 2 capsules 3 times a day.

10. _____ Apply a small amount of the ointment 3 times a day.

11. _____ If sore throat pain persists, contact your doctor.

12. _____ For relief of headache and muscle pain.

B Read the charts.

Modal: *Should*			
Subject	***Should***	**Base verb**	**Example sentence**
I, you, he, she, we, they	should	take	I **should** take two tablets.
		talk	He **should** talk to the doctor.
		take	You **should** take this medicine for a headache.
		swallow	They **should** swallow this tablet with water.

Modal: *Shouldn't*			
Subject	***Should***	**Base verb**	**Example sentence**
I, you, he, she, we, they	should not / shouldn't	take	You **shouldn't** take this pill with other medicine.
		chew	He **shouldn't** drink alcohol with this medicine.
		drink	She **shouldn't** chew this tablet.

C. Read the problems. Use the words to give advice.

1. I need some aspirin. (go to the drugstore)   You should go to the drugstore.

2. We are very tired. (sleep eight hours tonight) _____

3. Ricardo has a cough. (take some cough syrup) _____

4. I broke my arm. (go to the hospital) _____

5. You have a fever. (go to bed) _____

6. Luisa has a headache. (take some aspirin) _____

7. Those men smoke too much. (stop smoking) _____

8. My eyes hurt. (go to the optometrist) _____

D. Complete the sentences with *should* or *shouldn't*.

1. You _____ shouldn't _____ play soccer today. (no)

2. I _____ stop smoking. (yes)

3. Carla _____ eat fatty foods. (no)

4. You _____ take aspirin if you have the chicken pox. (no)

5. The children _____ have a checkup every year. (yes)

6. Ivan _____ take his medicine three times a day. (yes)

7. You _____ make an appointment with the doctor. (yes)

8. They _____ be nervous all the time. (no)

9. I _____ take some cough syrup for my cough. (yes)

10. We _____ drink too much coffee. (no)

E. Write some advice for a cold.

1. You should _____

2. _____

3. You shouldn't _____

4. _____

Health

CHALLENGE 5 ➤ Simple Past: Irregular Verbs

A Read the paragraph.

911 Operators and Emergencies

911 emergency is a very important number. Sometimes more calls come to the operators than they can answer. 911 operators have a difficult job. They have to decide which call is most important. People are often excited or nervous when they call. The operator should stay calm. People calling should explain the problem and give all the important information, including their name and address. The 911 operator should be patient. The operator's job is to call the fire department, the police, or a poison control center. Sometimes people call for things that are not emergencies. It is important to call 911 ONLY in the case of an emergency.

B Answer the questions about the paragraph.

1. What should the 911 operator do in case of an emergency?
   a. go home early
   b. call the fire department, the police, or a poison control center
   c. talk to the supervisor

2. What information should the caller give?
   a. his or her name and the address where the emergency is located
   b. his or her driver's license number
   c. the fire department or paramedics

C Read the chart.

Simple Past: Irregular Verbs		
Verbs with a spelling change in the simple past tense		
break – broke	find – found	sit – sat
buy – bought	get – got	sleep – slept
come – came	go – went	take – took
do – did	pay – paid	understand – understood
drink – drank	read – read*	wake – woke
drive – drove	say – said**	wear – wore
eat – ate	see – saw	write – wrote
*the past tense sounds like *red*	**said* rhymes with *red*	
Verbs with no change in the simple past tense		
hurt – hurt	put – put	cost – cost

D Complete each sentence with the simple past tense of the verb in parentheses.

EXAMPLE: I _____broke_____ (break) my arm last week.

1. My brother _____ (drive) to the hospital.

2. You _____ (wake) up at 7:00.

3. You _____ (go) to the doctor at noon.

4. Your parents _____ (buy) you some aspirin.

5. They _____ (come) to visit you.

6. Teresa _____ (do) some exercises.

7. She _____ (eat) a healthy breakfast.

8. Dan _____ (sleep) eight hours last night.

9. He _____ (take) some vitamins.

10. I _____ (get) sick yesterday.

11. My sister _____ (say) she was sick, too.

12. We _____ (drink) a lot of orange juice.

E Rewrite each sentence in the simple past tense.

EXAMPLE: I wake up at 6:00 A.M.   I woke up at 6:00 A.M.

1. My throat hurts.

2. You drive me to the doctor at noon.

3. The doctor says to take some medicine.

4. I get the medicine from the doctor.

5. You read the directions.

6. I take two teaspoons of the syrup.

7. I sleep for ten hours.

8. We eat a good breakfast.

9. My friends come to see me.

10. They buy me some flowers.

F Write a conversation about an emergency. Then, practice it with a classmate.

911 Operator: 911 operator. May I help you? _____

Caller: _____

911 Operator: _____

Caller: _____

911 Operator: _____

Caller: _____

911 Operator: _____

Caller: _____

911 Operator: _____

Simple Past: Irregular Verbs

Questions with Should

EXTENSION CHALLENGE 1 ➤ **Questions with *Should***

A Label the pictures with the ailments.

_____   _____   _____

_____   _____

B Write medication for each picture.

1. Alexi has a headache. _____aspirin_____

2. Mario has a stomachache. _____

3. Dalva has a toothache. _____

4. Gilberto has a backache. _____

5. Marie has a sore throat. _____

C Read the chart.

Questions with *Should*	
Yes/No Question	**Short answer**
Should I exercise every day?	Yes, you **should**. No, you **shouldn't**.
Should he **have** a checkup?	Yes, he **should**. No, he **shouldn't**.
Should we **buy** some vitamins?	Yes, we **should**. No, we **shouldn't**.
Information Question	**Answer**
Who **should I ask** about the medicine?	You **should** ask the doctor.
Where **should** she **buy** the cough syrup?	She **should** buy the cough syrup at the pharmacy.
Why **should** we **take** the pills?	We have a cough and a fever.
• For *Yes/No* questions and information questions, use *should* + the base form.	

D Use the words to write *yes/no* questions with *should.*

EXAMPLE: the / go / should / to / dentist / you   <u>Should you go to the dentist?</u>

1. coffee / should / drink / I   _____

2. three meals a day / should / eat / Eva   _____

3. reduce / should / the fever / the medicine   _____

4. a checkup / should / have / Mario   _____

5. you / chew / the tablets / should   _____

6. an appointment / make / they / should   _____

7. should / an ambulance / call / I   _____

8. should / smoking / stop / your parents   _____

E Read each statement. Then, write information questions.

EXAMPLE: You should exercise every day. (why)   <u>Why should I exercise every day?</u>

1. Your mother should lose weight. (how)   _____

2. Rosa should take her medicine. (when)   _____

3. You should run every day. (why)   _____

4. The children should play soccer. (where)   _____

5. We should visit today. (who)   _____

6. Tan and Diem should go to the dentist. (when)   _____

7. Vladimir should take aspirin. (why)   _____

8. I should eat tonight. (what)   _____

9. You should call in the morning. (who)   _____

10. We should call for an appointment. (where)   _____

F Use the information from Exercises A and B and write *yes/no* questions.

1. <u>Should Alexi take aspirin for a headache?</u>

2. _____

3. _____

4. _____

5. _____

EXTENSION CHALLENGE 2 ➤ **Simple Past: Questions**

A Read the conversation.

Doctor: Hello, Victor. How are you today?
Victor: I am very sick. I have chest pains
and a backache.
Doctor: Did you take your medicine today?
Victor: No, I don't like it.
Doctor: You have to take it. Please take
it when you get home.
Victor: Yes, doctor. I will.
Doctor: Did you exercise yesterday?
Victor: No.
Doctor: Did you eat well yesterday?
Victor: No.
Doctor: Did you get any rest.
Victor: No.
Doctor: Victor, to get better, you need
to follow the doctor's orders!

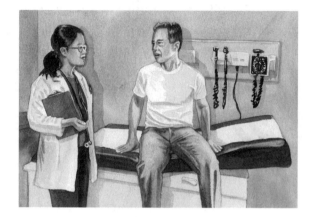

B Answer the questions.

1. How many hours do you think Victor should sleep? _____

2. How much do you think he should exercise? _____

3. How many meals should he eat? _____

C Read the charts.

Simple Past: Questions	
Yes/No Question	**Short answer**
Did you **exercise** yesterday?	Yes, I **did.** No, I **didn't.**
Did he **have** an earache?	Yes, he **did.** No, he **didn't.**
Did we **buy** any aspirin?	Yes, we **did.** No, we **didn't.**
• For *yes/no* questions in the simple past tense (regular or irregular verbs), use *did* + the base form.	
Information Question	**Answer**
Where **did** you **play** soccer yesterday?	I played soccer in the park.
How **did** she **get** to the doctor's office?	She took the bus.
When **did** they **have** an appointment?	They had an appointment at 3:00.
• For information questions in the simple past tense, use *did* + the base form.	

D **Write *yes/no* questions and a short answer.**

EXAMPLE: *Q:* (she / fever) <u>Did she have a fever?</u>

  A: No, <u>she didn't</u>. She had a cold.

1. *Q:* (you / headache) _____

   A: No, _____. I had a stomachache.

2. *Q:* (Rosa / Monday / exercise) _____

   A: No, _____. Rosa exercised on Friday.

3. *Q:* (you / dentist) _____

   A: No, _____. I went to the doctor.

4. *Q:* (they / warnings) _____

   A: No, _____. They read the directions.

5. *Q:* (you / orange juice) _____

   A: No, _____. We drank a lot of water.

6. *Q:* (the cat / its foot) _____

   A: No, _____. The cat broke its leg.

E **Use the words to write information questions in the simple past.**

EXAMPLE:

last year / did / when / see / the doctor / we   <u>When did we see the doctor last year?</u>

1. did / what / the doctor / say   _____

2. pay / did / you / how   _____

3. buy / Marina / where / did / the medicine   _____

4. she / did / who / the pills / for / buy   _____

5. smoking / when / your parents / did / stop   _____

6. every / did / why / exercise / day / they   _____

F **Write a new conversation with a doctor. Practice with a partner.**

Student A: _____

Student B: _____

Student A: _____

Student B: _____

Student A: _____

Student B: _____

Student A: _____

Student B: _____

Work, Work, Work

CHALLENGE 1 ➤ Future: *Will*

A Study Vincent's evaluation.

EVALUATION

Date: August 10, 2009	Name: Vincent Nunez			Supervisor: Betty Moore			
1. Comes to work on time	S	G	NI	4. Works well with a team	S	G	NI
2. Follows instructions	S	G	NI	5. Understands the job	S	G	NI
3. Helps others	S	G	NI	6. Has a positive attitude	S	G	NI

S=Superior   G=Good   NI=Needs Improvement

Betty Moore

B Read the conversation below and mark the evaluation with *S*, *G*, and *NI*.

Supervisor: Vincent, I want to go over your evaluation.

Vincent: OK, I try to do a good job.

Supervisor: Yes I see that every day. I have given you a "*superior*" for coming to work on time and understanding the job. I have also marked "*good*" for attitude.

Vincent: Why do I not have a "*superior*" for attitude?

Supervisor: . . . because you don't help other employees or want to work in a team. See, both of these areas are "*needs improvement.*"

Vincent: Is working in a team important for my job?

Supervisor: Absolutely! It is important for every job.

Vincent: I will improve. I will begin today to work with the other employees.

Supervisor: I was sure you would. That is why I give you a "*superior*" for following instructions.

C Read the charts.

Future: *Will* (Affirmative)			
Subject	***Will***	**Base verb**	**Example sentence**
I, you, he, she, we, they	will	come	I **will** come to class on time.
		listen	You **will** listen carefully and follow instructions.
		help	They **will** help other students.
		work	We **will** work hard.
		have	He **will** have a positive attitude.

Future: *Will* (Negative)			
Subject	***Will***	**Base verb**	**Example sentence**
I, you, he, she, we, they	will not (won't)	come	I **won't** come to class late.
		leave	I **won't** leave class early.
		forget	I **won't** forget my homework.

D **Circle the correct future verb form.**

1. Vincent (will work) / will working on a team in the future.

2. Raquel **is listen** / **will listen** to the teacher next week.

3. Marie and Raquel **is coming** / **will come** to class on time tomorrow.

4. I **will follow** / **will following** instructions at work in the future.

5. We **will leave** / **are leave** class at 6:00 P.M. tomorrow.

6. You **not will have** / **will not have** a better attitude after you eat.

7. She **wills need** / **will need** assistance from another worker.

8. Jean **won't** / **wills not** smoke at work.

9. Lien and Duong **are having** / **will have** homework.

10. Tuba **will leaves** / **will leave** for Texas in the morning.

E **Rewrite the statements in the future affirmative and negative.**

1. Lydia comes to work on time.
   a. Lydia will come to work on time.
   b. Lydia won't come to work on time.

2. The Nguyen brothers follow instructions well.
   a. _____
   b. _____

3. I help others at every opportunity.
   a. _____
   b. _____

4. We work well in a team.
   a. _____
   b. _____

F **Check (✓) what you will do in the future.**

☐ study English   ☐ work tomorrow   ☐ do my homework
☐ listen in class   ☐ come to school on time ☐ smoke in class

G **Write one negative and one affirmative sentence with information from Exercise F.**

1. _____
2. _____

Work, Work, Work

CHALLENGE 2 ➤ Modal: *Can* (Ability)

Modal: *Can* (Ability) *(side tab)*

A Identify jobs and job skills.

Name: Alana Kim

SKILLS

Typing: 45 wpm   Languages: German
Other Skills: file, use a copy machine, manage an office, write business letters

JOB HISTORY

Position	Company	Duties
Office Manager	Barcelona Tile	manage paperwork, set appointments, supervise three employees
Administrative Assistant	Jocelyn's Jewelry Emporium	type letters, answer phones, file papers, speak to customers
File Clerk	Jocelyn's Jewelry Emporium	type letters, file papers

B Make a list of ten things Alana can do with information from Exercise A.

1. use a copy machine
2. supervise employees
3. _____
4. _____
5. _____

6. _____
7. _____
8. _____
9. _____
10. _____

C Read the chart.

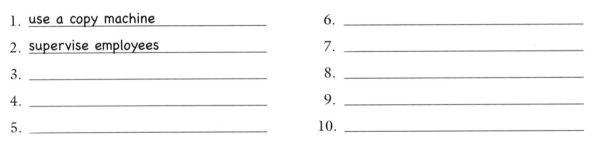

Modal: *Can* (Ability)			
	Subject	*Can*	Base verb	Example sentence
Affirmative	I	can	type	I **can** type 60 words a minute.
	he, she, it	can	use	He/ She **can** use a computer.
	we	can	fix	We **can** fix things around the house.
Negative	you	**cannot**	speak	You **cannot** speak Spanish.
	they	**can't**	turn	They **can't** turn on the copier.

• The negative of *can* is *cannot.* The contraction is *can't.*

D Write what these people *can* and *can't* do.

EXAMPLE: Kenji _____can_____ use a computer. (yes)

1. I _____ type quickly. (no)

2. Marie _____ speak Japanese. (no)

3. Anya and Ivan _____ use e-mail. (yes)

4. You _____ put the paper in the printer. (no)

5. We _____ work well together. (yes)

6. I _____ turn on the fax machine. (no)

7. They _____ understand Chinese. (yes)

8. We _____ drive a car. (yes)

9. Sam _____ speak English well. (no)

10. Gilberto _____ prepare food. (yes)

11. I _____ cook well. (no)

12. You _____ teach English. (yes)

E Use the words to write about what people *can* and *cannot* do.

EXAMPLE: speak / cannot / Russian / I   _____I cannot speak Russian._____

1. can / soccer / you / play   _____

2. Sara / the piano / can't / play   _____

3. draw / well / cannot / we   _____

4. can / the house / things / around / Ivan / fix   _____

5. the computer / Dalva / use / can   _____

6. a truck / you / drive / can't   _____

7. the children / swim / can   _____

8. Spanish / teach / cannot / I   _____

9. cook / food / Mexican / Mario / can   _____

10. can't / Chinese / we / understand   _____

F Check (✓) what you can do.

☐ type
☐ listen in class

☐ answer phones
☐ take messages

☐ do my homework
☐ file papers

G Write sentences about what you *can* and *can't* do using the information from Exercise F.

1. (can) _____

2. (can) _____

3. (can't) _____

4. (can't) _____

Work, Work, Work

CHALLENGE 3 ➤ Questions with *May* and *Can*

A Read the classified ads.

★ **DRIVER NEEDED** ★

1 yr. exp, f/t or p/t, gd bnfts, we will train, appl avail. $12/hr. Call 555-7467 M–F, 8–6. **Qualifications:** speak English, drive a truck.

Hairstylist

Must know all styles, $15/hr, p/t, 3 yrs. exp req., app. in person. Call for appt. 555-3456. **Qualifications:** work on weekends, use a cash register.

ASSEMBLY WORKER

f/t, no exp nec., gd benefits, opp. for advancement, $7.00 to start. Call 555-3456. **Qualifications:** speak English, work at night.

☞ **Secretary** ☜

Exp. nec., p/t only, gd pay and bnfts, vacation and travel, $18/hr. Call 555-9845. **Qualifications:** speak Spanish and English, type 60 words per minute.

B Complete the chart with information from the classified ads above.

Position	Experience?	F/T or P/T	Pay
Driver	1 yr.		
Assembly worker			
Hairstylist			
Secretary			

C Read the chart.

Questions with *May* and *Can*			
Can	**Subject**	**Base verb**	**Example question and answer**
can	I, you, he, she, it, we, they	type	**Can** you type letters? Yes, I can.
		drive	**Can** they drive a car? No, they can't.
		understand	**Can** she understand English? Yes, she can.
		work	**Can** I work on Saturdays? Yes, you can.
		cook	**Can** he cook breakfast? No, he can't.
		clean	**Can** we clean on the weekend? Yes, you can.
		talk	**Can** you talk to customers? No, you can't.

D Write *yes/no* questions to ask what people can do.

1. Anya and Ivan / work on Saturday <u>Can Anya and Ivan work on Saturday?</u>

2. Diem / drive a car _____

3. I / file those letters _____

4. you / send me a resume _____

5. we / talk about the job _____

6. Don / give me his application _____

E List the qualifications for the jobs in the classified ads in Exercise A.

Driver	Assembly Worker	Hairstylist	Secretary
speak English			

F Write interview questions for the people indicated with information from the chart.

1. **Driver**

   (Mario) <u>Can Mario speak English?</u> _____

   (You) _____

2. **Assembly Worker**

   (Anya) _____

   (Peter and Jane) _____

3. **Hairstylist**

   (You) _____

   (Kevin) _____

4. **Secretary**

   (You) _____

   (Pilar) _____

G Interview three students for the jobs listed in the classified ads in Exercise A.

EXAMPLE:
Student A: Can you speak English?
Student B: Yes, a little.
Student A: Can you drive a truck?
Student B: No, but I can learn.

Work, Work, Work

CHALLENGE 4 ➤ Simple Past

A Read Hakim's job history.

Employment History *(Please list most recent position first.)*

Employer	Position	from Dates to		Reason for leaving
Right Value Hotel	3. Hotel manager	02-2008	10-2008	I moved
Right Value Hotel	2. Supervisor	05-01	07-2007	promotion
Right Value Hotel	1. Housekeeper	10-99	05-01	promotion

B Complete the time line.

1999	2000	2001	2002	2003	2004	2005	2006	2007	2008

3.

2.

1.   housekeeper

C Answer the questions about the job history.

1. How long did he work for Right Value Hotel? _____9_____ (years/months)

2. How long did he work as a housekeeper? _____ (years/months)

3. How long did he work as a supervisor? _____ (years/months)

4. How long did he work as a manager? _____ (months)

D Read the chart.

Simple Past	
Negative forms of regular and irregular verbs (except *be*)	
I **didn't work** in the evenings.	We **didn't have** a paid vacation.
Dalva **didn't know** how to type.	You **didn't turn off** the computer.
• For all forms of regular and irregular verbs (except *be*), use *did not* (*didn't*) + base.	
Negative forms of *be*	
I **wasn't** at work today. He/She/It **wasn't** friendly.	We **weren't** happy. You **weren't** in the hospital. They **weren't** at the front desk.
• For the verb *be*, use *was not* (*wasn't*) and *were not* (*weren't*).	

E Bubble in the correct negative form to complete each sentence.

EXAMPLE: They _____ the phone. ○ didn't answered ● didn't answer

1. I _____ an administrative assistant. ○ weren't ○ wasn't

2. Last year, Marie _____ health insurance. ○ didn't have ○ doesn't have

3. The resumes _____ on my desk. ○ weren't ○ wasn't

4. Geraldo _____ as a gardener. ○ not work ○ didn't work

5. Marie _____ French at her old job. ○ didn't speak ○ didn't spoke

6. You _____ about my new job. ○ didn't ask ○ didn't asked

7. We _____ the job ads yesterday. ○ don't read ○ didn't read

8. I _____ out the job application. ○ didn't fill ○ didn't fills

F Complete each sentence with the negative form of the underlined verb.

EXAMPLE: Dalva worked at a hotel. She _____didn't work_____ at a hospital.

1. She checked the reservations. She _____ the job applications.

2. I typed letters all day. I _____ e-mails.

3. I was available for work on Saturday. I _____ available for work on Sunday.

4. You were interested in a full-time job. You _____ interested in a part-time job.

5. You knew how to use the fax machine. You _____ how to use the shredder.

6. We were at the copier. We _____ at the printer.

7. They offered free training. They _____ health insurance.

8. Youssouf kept all the files. He _____ all the software programs.

9. He was at the office all day. He _____ at home.

10. My sister applied for a job as a legal assistant. She _____ for a job as a clerk.

G Rewrite the sentences about Exercise A in the negative.

1. Hakim was a hairstylist from 1999 to 2001.

   Hakim wasn't a hairstylist from 1999 to 2001.

2. He managed the hotel for three years.

   _____

3. He answered the phones in the office in 2002.

   _____

4. Hakim and the other housekeepers worked for free.

   _____

Work, Work, Work

CHALLENGE 5 ➤ Imperatives

| choose | close | connect | press/enter | record | turn off | turn on | ~~open~~ |

A Write the words under the pictures.

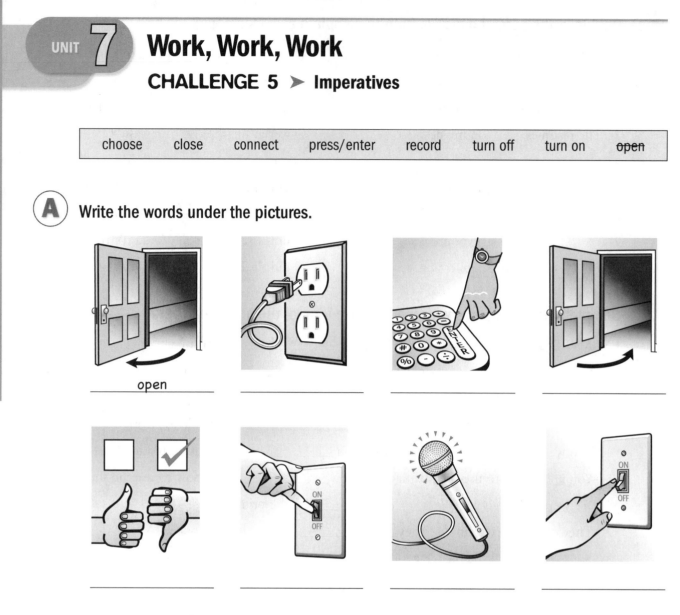

open

_____

_____

_____

_____

_____

_____

_____

B Read the chart.

Imperatives	
Affirmative imperative	**Negative imperative**
Write your name on the application.	**Don't write** your age.
Press the green button.	**Don't press** the red button.
Be helpful at work.	**Don't be** late for work.

- The imperative uses the base form of the verb.
- The subject is **you**, but it is not included.
- The negative imperative is *do not* + base form. The contraction is *don't*.
- Imperatives give warnings, directions, or suggestions.
- Use an exclamation mark (!) if the feeling is very strong.

C Circle the correct imperative sentence.

1. (Turn on the copier.) / You can turn on the copier. / Turns on the copier.

2. Doesn't connect the printer. / Don't connect the printer. / Connecting the printer.

3. Enters the information. / Enter the information. / enter the information.

4. Jose, records a message. / Please, recording a message. / Please, record a message.

5. Choose the answer. / Chooses the answer. / Is choosing an answer.

6. Doesn't close the lid. / Are not close the lid. / Don't close the lid.

7. Open the container. / Opens the container. / You can open the container.

8. Turning off the machine. / Don't off the machine. / Turn off the machine.

D Make each sentence negative using the words given.

EXAMPLE:

Record the new message. (old message)   <u>Don't record the old message.</u>

1. Turn on the new copier. (broken copier) _____

2. Put the paper in the top. (bottom) _____

3. Turn off the shredder. (printer) _____

4. Press the stop button. (start button) _____

5. Enter a number. (name) _____

6. Wait for an answer. (beep) _____

7. Connect the printer to the computer. (fax) _____

8. Place the paper in the top slot. (middle slot) _____

9. Keep the printer near the copier. (phone) _____

10. Turn off the copier at night. (in the morning) _____

E Write directions for a microwave oven.

Microwave Instructions

Work, Work, Work

EXTENSION CHALLENGE 1 ➤ Regular Past Tense: Spelling

A Read the job history.

JOB APPLICATION

PERSONAL INFORMATION

Name: *Arthur Frank* Position: *Nurse* Phone: *(731)555-9835*

EMPLOYMENT HISTORY *(Please list most recent positions first.)*

Employer	Position	from Dates to		Reason for leaving
Speedy Tune-Up	Manager	10-2008	Present	Want new experience
Speedy Tune-Up	Mechanic	3-1998	10-2008	New position
Ned's Auto Shop	Mechanic	10-1997	3-1998	New position/Better pay

B Answer the questions about the job history in Exercise A.

1. How long did Arthur work for Ned's Auto Shop? ____6 months____

2. Why did he change jobs? _____

3. How long did he work for Speedy Tune-Up? _____

4. What was his last job? _____

C Read the chart.

Regular Past Tense: Spelling		
Rule	**Base**	**Past Tense**
To form the simple past tense of regular verbs, add *-ed* to the base form.	work	work**ed**
Irregular spellings in the simple past tense		
• If the base verb ends in **e**, add *-d*.	manage	mana**ged**
• If the base verb ends in a *consonant* + **y**, change the **y** to **i** and add *-ed*.	study	stud**ied**
• If the base verbs ends in a *vowel* + **y**, add *-ed*.	play	play**ed**
• For one-syllable words, double the final consonant if the base ends in consonant-vowel-consonant.	stop	stop**ped**
Exception: Don't double **w** or **x**.	show	show**ed**
• For two-syllable words that end in *consonant-vowel-consonant*, double the final consonant only if the last syllable is stressed.	prefer	prefer**red**
• If the last syllable is not stressed, do not double the final consonant.	happen	happen**ed**

D Write the simple past tense of these verbs. Some have spelling changes.

EXAMPLE: stay _____ stayed _____

1. fix _____   6. drop _____

2. use _____   7. permit _____

3. remember _____   8. open _____

4. cry _____   9. carry _____

5. listen _____   10. enjoy _____

E Fill in the blanks with the simple past.

EXAMPLE: I _____ started _____ (start) my job in July.

1. Anya _____ (deliver) the mail this morning.

2. That man _____ (chew) gum during his interview.

3. I _____ (manage) 100 employees.

4. The cook _____ (chop) vegetables for the soup.

5. The secretary _____ (show) the letter to the manager.

6. The custodians never _____ (clean) the halls.

7. Ben and Luiz _____ (decide) to open a restaurant.

8. They _____ (apply) for jobs in our company.

9. We _____ (stop) working at 6:00.

10. The carpenter _____ (drop) the hammer.

F Complete the history about someone you know.

EMPLOYMENT HISTORY		Dates		(Please list most recent positions first.)
Employer	Position	from	to	Reason for leaving

G What are the responsibilities of the job above? Write verbs that describe the duties or responsibilities in the past tense.

_____   _____   _____   _____

_____   _____   _____   _____

Work, Work, Work

EXTENSION CHALLENGE 2 ➤ Simple Past: Irregular Verbs

Simple Past: Irregular Verbs

A Write the number of the responsibilities next to the job title.

| 1. drives a truck | 3. builds houses | 5. delivers packages | 7. fixes cars |
| 2. makes cabinets | 4. helps students | 6. types letters | 8. cleans offices |

___2___ carpenter _____ teacher _____ custodian _____ delivery person

_____ driver _____ mechanic _____ office worker _____ construction worker

B Read the chart.

Base form	Past form	Base form	Past form	Base form	Past form
become	became	give	gave	see	saw
begin	began	go	went	sell	sold
break	broke	grow	grew	send	sent
bring	brought	hang	hung	sing	sang
build	built	have	had	sit	sat
buy	bought	hear	heard	sleep	slept
catch	caught	hurt	hurt	speak	spoke
choose	chose	know	knew	spend	spent
come	came	leave	left	stand	stood
cost	cost	lose	lost	sweep	swept
cut	cut	make	made	take	took
do	did	meet	met	teach	taught
draw	drew	pay	paid	tell	told
drink	drank	put	put	think	thought
drive	drove	quit	quit	throw	threw
eat	ate	read	read*	understand	understood
feel	felt	ride	rode	wake	woke
find	found	ring	rang	wear	wore
forget	forgot	run	ran	write	wrote
get	got	say	said		

• Many verbs are irregular in the simple past tense. You need to memorize these verbs.

* The past form *read* rhymes with *red*.

C Complete each sentence with the simple past.

EXAMPLE: I _____wrote_____ (write) a letter to the manager.

1. We _____ (build) this road last year.

2. I _____ (hear) about the benefits.

3. We _____ (buy) suits for the interview.

4. She _____ (give) me my paycheck.

5. I _____ (hurt) my knee at work.

6. Victor _____ (wear) a hard hat.

7. She _____ (become) a doctor.

8. The custodians _____ (throw) out the trash.

9. My boss _____ (catch) a cold.

10. Beth _____ (read) her evaluation.

11. He _____ (find) a great job.

12. She _____ (know) every coworker.

13. I _____ (put) the package over there.

14. We _____ (find) the office keys.

15. He _____ (pay) the delivery person.

16. David _____ (sell) his first TV.

17. Marcia _____ (run) to the bus station.

18. I _____ (bring) coffee to the meeting.

19. We _____ (speak) to the supervisor.

20. Anita _____ (quit) her job.

D Use the simple past to describe the jobs below.

1. John was a construction worker. He _____built_____ homes.

2. Maria was a driver. She _____ a truck.

3. Huong was a carpenter. He _____ furniture.

4. Maribel was a gardener. She _____ flowers.

5. She was a singer. She _____.

6. He was a custodian. He _____ the floor.

7. They were artists. They _____ pictures.

8. He was an author. He _____ books.

UNIT 8 Goals and Lifelong Learning

CHALLENGE 1 ➤ Future Infinitives and *Be going to*

A Read the goals.

go to college	learn English in school	buy a house
get married	get a high school diploma	get a job
have children	be a doctor	keep a job

B Write the goals from Exercise A in the correct column.

Personal and Family	Vocational (Work)	Academic (Educational)
buy a house		

C Read the charts.

Express Future Plans: *want to, hope to, plan to*		
Subject	**Verb**	**Infinitive (*to* + base)**
I, you, we, they	hope, want, plan	to { **study** in school for three years
he, she	hopes, wants, plans	**graduate** from college **get** married **be** a doctor }

Express Future Plans: *Be going to*			
Subject	***Be going to***	**Base verb**	**Information**
I	am going to	get	a high school diploma
you, we, they	are going to	participate	in my child's school
he, she	is going to	buy	a house

want to	*hope to*	*plan to*	*be going to*
less definite		——————————————▶	more definite

D Write the correct verb to express the future.

1. I _____ want to get _____ (want / get) a better job.

2. Marie _____ (be going / study) medicine.

3. We _____ (hope / graduate) from the university.

4. Mario _____ (plan / learn) English at school.

5. Miguel and Anita _____ (be going / become) citizens.

6. You _____ (want / return) to your country.

7. My sister _____ (be going / get) married.

8. I _____ (plan / buy) a house and a car.

9. Many students _____ (be going / have) good careers.

10. We _____ (hope / be) successful.

E Write the sentences from definite to less definite.

I hope to learn English.	I want to study music.
~~I am going to get a diploma.~~	I plan to be a teacher.

definite _____ I am going to get a diploma. _____

_____

_____

less definite _____

F Complete the sentences about you.

1. I hope to _____

2. I plan to _____

3. I am going to _____

4. I want to _____

G Complete the sentences about a classmate.

1. He hopes to _____

2. He plans to _____

3. He is going to _____

4. He wants to _____

Goals and Lifelong Learning

CHALLENGE 2 ➤ *Because* and Adverbial Clauses

Because and Adverbial Clauses

A Match each question with the reason. Write the correct letter next to each question.

___b___ 1. Why does Maria want to go to college?

_____ 2. Why is Arthur learning English?

_____ 3. Why is Chau happy today?

_____ 4. Why are John and Neil going to a trade school?

a. He graduated from college.

b. She wants to study nursing.

c. They plan to be mechanics.

d. He needs it to speak to his boss.

B Rewrite the questions in Exercise A as statements.

1. Maria wants to go to college. _____

2. _____

3. _____

4. _____

C Read the chart.

Because and Adverbial Clauses			
		Reason	
Statement		**Subject + verb**	**Information**
Maria plans to go to college	because	she wants	to be a nurse
Lien hopes to learn English better		she plans	to go to college

Examples: Maria plans to go to college **because** she wants to be a nurse.

Lien hopes to learn English **because** she plans to go to college.

Usage:

• Usually you do not write a comma after or before *because*.

• A subject always follows *because*.

Combine each sentence with a reason from the box using *because*.

She needs help with the homework.	~~He wants to get a better job.~~
You want to learn quickly.	I want to prepare for the test.
She wants to be a doctor.	They hope to be teachers.

1. John is studying English.

   John is studying English because he wants to get a better job.

2. Karen talks to the teacher.

   _____

3. Annabel plans to go to medical school.

   _____

4. Gilberto and Mario learn math.

   _____

5. I am going to study all night.

   _____

6. You listen carefully.

   _____

Use Exercises A and B to write sentences with *because*.

1. Maria wants to go to college because she wants to study nursing.
2. _____
3. _____
4. _____

F **Complete the sentences about your goals.**

1. I am studying English because _____.

2. I hope to _____ because _____.

3. I plan to _____ because _____.

4. I am going to _____ because _____.

Goals and Lifelong Learning

CHALLENGE 3 ➤ Future: *Will*

A Read Gilberto's time line.

2009	**2011**	**2012**	**2014**	**2016**	**2018**
work in my father's restaurant	cook new foods in my father's restaurant	buy a restaurant and serve international food	find a business partner	find another business partner	hire managers for all restaurants
go to cooking school	save money		start a second restaurant	start another restaurant	

Remember:

want to	*hope to*	*plan to*	*be going to*
less definite			→ more definite

B Write Gilberto's plans below. Do you think his plans are very definite or not very definite? Use *wants to, hopes to, plans to,* or *is going to.*

1. Gilberto is going to work in his father's restaurant in 2009. _____

2. _____

3. _____

4. _____

5. _____

6. _____

7. _____

8. _____

9. _____

10. _____

C Read the chart.

Future: *Will*			
Subject	***Will***	**Base verb**	**Information**
I, you,		go	to school for two more years
he, she, it,	will	study	English this year
we, they		be	a nurse
want to	*hope to*	*plan to*	*be going to* *will*
less definite			→ very definite

D Rewrite the sentences using *will* to express future.

1. Ahmed goes to a trade school. <u>Ahmed will go to a trade school.</u>

2. I have a new job. _____

3. Lien is a counselor. _____

4. I need a part-time job. _____

5. We graduate in the spring. _____

6. Mario owns an auto repair business. _____

7. Martina and Ana study accounting. _____

8. We save money. _____

9. You work in a library. _____

10. I apply for a library card. _____

E Write the correct verb to express the future.

1. Gilberto _____<u>hopes to have</u>_____ (hope / have) three restaurants by 2016.

2. Gilberto and Francisco _____ (plan / work) together.

3. We _____ (will / study) cooking in 2009.

4. Gilberto _____ (will / go) to cooking school.

5. Gilberto and Angela _____ (hope / get) married in 2012.

6. I _____ (be going / see) Gilberto soon.

F Make your own time line and tell a partner about your plans for the future.

2009	2011	2013
2015	2017	2019

Goals and Lifelong Learning

CHALLENGE 4 ➤ Simple Past with *so*

Simple Past with *so*

A Look at the problems and solutions.

Hector's problems	Solutions				
	asked a friend	called the police	went to school	asked the teacher	looked in a newspaper
He didn't speak English.			X		
He didn't have a job.					X
He needed to find a home for his family.	X				
He had an emergency.		X			

B Write sentences following the example.

1. Hector asked a friend because he needed to find a home for his family.

2. _____

3. _____

4. _____

C Read the chart.

Simple Past with *so*							
Base	Affirmative	Negative		Base	Affirmative	Negative	
		didn't	base			*didn't*	base
ask	asked	didn't	ask	go	went	didn't	go
look	looked		look	have	had	didn't	have
talk	talked		talk	speak	spoke	didn't	speak
call	called		call	know	knew	didn't	know

Usage: a. and b. mean the same.

a. He talked to the teacher because <u>he didn't speak English.</u>

b. <u>He didn't speak English,</u> *so* he talked to the teacher.

a. He looked in the newspaper because <u>he didn't have a job.</u>

b. <u>He didn't have a job,</u> *so* he looked in the newspaper.

Tuba's problem	Solution		
	looked in the phone book	talked to a counselor	asked the teacher
She didn't know where to find information about citizenship.		X	
She didn't know how to read a bus schedule.			X
She needed to find a school for her children.	X		

D Look at the problems and solutions. Then, write three sentences with *because* about the problems and solutions and three sentences with *so*.

because

1. Tuba talked to a counselor because she didn't know where to find information about citizenship.

2. She asked the teacher because _____

3. _____

so

1. _____

2. _____

3. _____

E Rewrite the sentences in Exercise B with *so* in place of *because*.

1. Hector needed to find a home for his family, so he asked a friend.

2. _____

3. _____

4. _____

F Write two of your problems and solutions. Then, tell a classmate.

Your problems	Solutions
1.	
2.	

Goals and Lifelong Learning

CHALLENGE 5 ➤ Transition Words

Transition Words *(sidebar)*

A Read the paragraph about Kenji's goals.

My Goals
I have many goals for the next five years. Right now, I am studying at Lincoln Adult School. <u>First</u>, in 2009 and 2010 I will learn English. I will come to school every day. <u>Next</u>, in 2011 I hope to get a high school diploma and register at the local college. <u>Then</u>, in 2012 I plan to find a job. <u>Finally</u>, in 2013 I will graduate with an A.A. degree and get a better job.

B Complete the chart with the information from Exercise A.

2009	2010	2011	2012	2013
I will learn English.				

C Read the chart.

Transition Words in Sentences		
With numbers	**Without numbers**	**Example sentence**
First (First of all)	First	First of all, I went to town. **First**, I went to town.
Second	Next	Second, I ate. / **Next**, I ate.
Third	Then	Third, I saw a movie. / **Then**, I saw a movie.
	After that	After that, I had a soda.
Finally / Lastly	Finally	Lastly, I went home. / **Finally**, I went home.

- Do not use numbers as transition words if there are more than four steps.
- When not using numbers, *next, then,* and *after that* can be used in any order to describe more than one step.
- Always finish with the words *finally* or *lastly*.

Gilberto's Plan

2009	2011	2012	2014	2016	2018
work in my father's restaurant go to cooking school	cook new foods in my father's restaurant save money	buy a restaurant and serve international food	find a business partner start a second restaurant	find another business partner start another restaurant	hire managers for all restaurants

 Read Gilberto's time line. Write complete sentences about his plans.

1. Gilberto will work in his father's restaurant. _____
2. _____
3. _____
4. _____
5. _____
6. _____
7. _____
8. _____
9. _____
10. _____

E Write a paragraph with all the sentences in Exercise D. Use transition words that are not numbers.

Gilberto's Goals

Goals and Lifelong Learning

EXTENSION CHALLENGE 1 ➤ *Yes/No Questions and Will*

Yes/No Questions and Will

A Look at the information below. Write what you *will do*, what you *plan to do*, what you *hope to do*, and what you *won't do*.

1. learn English <u>I will learn English.</u>

2. get married _____

3. graduate from college _____

4. make a lot of money _____

5. be successful _____

6. have children _____

7. get a new job _____

8. help my family learn English _____

9. buy a home _____

10. send my children to a good school _____

B Read the chart.

Yes/No Questions with *Will*		
Statement	**Question**	**Answer**
I will be rich some day.	**Will** I **be** rich some day?	Yes, you will. No, you won't.
You will start college next year.	**Will** you **start** college next year?	Yes, I will. No, I won't.
He will find a job.	**Will** he **find** a job?	Yes, he will. No, he won't.
She will get some advice.	**Will** she **get** some advice?	Yes, she will. No, she won't.
It will be closed.	**Will** it **be** closed?	Yes, it will. No, it won't.
We will work together.	**Will** we **work** together?	Yes, we will. No, we won't.
They will handle the money.	**Will** they **handle** the money?	Yes, they will. No, they won't.

C Roberto has questions about his English class. Write short answers.

EXAMPLE: Will the class start at 7:00?　　Yes, <u>it will.</u>

1. Will Miss Clark teach the class?　　Yes, _____

2. Will we study grammar?　　Yes, _____

3. Will you teach us new vocabulary?　　Yes, _____

4. Will I need a computer?　　No, _____

5. Will the students work together?　　Yes, _____

6. Will my wife and I be in the same class?　　No, _____

D Use the words to write short conversations using *will*.

EXAMPLE:

A: (you / go / trade school / in the fall) <u>Will you go to trade school in the fall?</u>

B: No. (I / go / next spring) <u>I'll go next spring.</u>

1. *A:* (you / apply for / that job) _____

　 B: No. (I / apply [*negative*]) _____ I don't have experience.

2. *A:* (your sister / get / a bachelor's degree) _____

　 B: No. (she / finish / her GED / first) _____

3. *A:* (you / practice / your vocabulary / later) _____

　 B: Yes. (Manuel / help / me / study) _____

4. *A:* (Nubar / study / with us / tonight) _____

　 B: No. (he / have [*negative*] / time) _____

5. *A:* (you / change / your goals) _____

　 B: No. (I / quit [*negative*]) _____

E Write questions for the information in Exercise A.

1. <u>Will you learn English?</u>

2. _____

3. _____

4. _____

5. _____

6. _____

7. _____

8. _____

F Ask a partner the questions in Exercise E.

UNIT 8 Goals and Lifelong Learning

EXTENSION CHALLENGE 2 ➤ *Will* and *Be going to:* Information Questions

A Read the plans.

1. I am going to talk to my teacher <u>in the morning</u>.

2. I will go to the library <u>every Saturday for three weeks</u>.

3. She is going to have <u>three children</u>.

4. He will help with the children <u>tomorrow</u>.

5. They will study and get a <u>high school diploma</u>.

6. He will be a doctor in <u>five years</u>.

B Put the number in the correct column.

Short-term goals	Long-term goals
1. talk to the teacher	

C Read the chart.

Will/Be going to: Information Questions	
Wh- word + *will* + subject + base verb	**Wh- word + *be* + subject + *going to* + base verb**
What **will** you do tomorrow?	What **are** you **going to** do tomorrow?
What time **will** she leave?	What time **is** she **going to** leave?
How **will** you pay for school?	How **are** you **going to** pay for school?
When **will** they arrive?	When **are** they **going to** arrive?
How much time **will** the students have?	How much time **are** the students **going to** have?
How long **will** they stay?	How long **are** they **going to** stay?
How often **will** you take a trip?	How often **are** you **going to** take a trip?
Where **will** she live?	Where **is** she **going to** live?

D Choose the correct form of the verb.

EXAMPLE: Where _____ he going to find a job?   ● is   ○ are

1. How often will she _____ home?   ○ calls   ○ call

2. How many questions are going _____ on the test?   ○ be   ○ to be

3. How _____ I going to save money for a car?   ○ am   ○ is

4. How much time is the interview going _____ ?   ○ take   ○ to take

5. When will she _____ the bills?   ○ pay   ○ to pay

6. What are they going _____ after graduation?   ○ do   ○ to do

7. What time will the class _____ ?   ○ to start   ○ start

8. How much _____ the books going to cost?   ○ is   ○ are

E Jin wants to study in the United States. His father is asking him questions about his plans. Use the words to write questions with *will* or *going to*.

EXAMPLE: where / stay   <u>Where will you stay? or Where are you going to stay?</u>

1. what / you / study   _____

2. how long / you / stay / there   _____

3. how much / school / cost   _____

4. how / we / pay for it   _____

5. where / you / live   _____

6. what / your teachers / say   _____

7. when / the course / start   _____

8. when / you / apply   _____

F Write questions for the information in Exercise A. Use the underlined words to choose the information word.

1. <u>When are you going to talk to your teacher?</u> _____

2. _____

3. _____

4. _____

5. _____

6. _____

➤ GLOSSARY OF GRAMMAR TERMS

adjective	a word that describes a noun (Example: the _red_ hat)
adverb	a word that modifies a verb, adjective, or another adverb (Example: She eats _quickly_.)
affirmative	not negative and not a question (Example: _I like him._)
animate/inanimate	objects that act or move (Example: _teacher_ or _water_) / objects that don't act or move (Example: _book_ or _desk_)
apostrophe	a punctuation mark that shows missing letters in contractions or possession (Example: _It's_ or _Jim's_)
article	words used before a noun (Example: _a_, _an_, _the_)
base form	the main form of the verb, used without _to_ (Example: _be_, _have_, _study_)
comma	the punctuation mark (,) used to indicate a pause or separation (Example: I live in an apartment, and you live in a house.)
complement	a word or words that add to or complete an idea after the verb (Example: He _is happy_.)
conjugation	the forms of a verb (Example: I _am_, You _are_, We _are_, They _are_, He _is_, She _is_, It _is_)
conjunction	a type of word that joins other words or phrases (Example: Maria _and_ Gilberto)
consonant	any letter of the alphabet that is not a vowel (Example: B, C, D, F . . .)
continuous form	a verb form that expresses action during time (Example: He _is shopping_.)
contraction	shortening of a word, syllable, or word group by omission of a sound or letter (Example: It is = _It's_, does not = _doesn't_)
count nouns	nouns that can be counted by number (Example: one _apple_, two _apples_)
definite article	use of _the_ when a noun is known to speaker and listener (Example: I know _the_ store.)
exclamation mark	a punctuation symbol marking surprise or emotion (Example: Hello_!_)
formal	polite or respectful language (Example: _Could_ you _please_ give me that?)
future	a verb form in the future tense (Example: I _will_ study at that school next year.)
imperative	a command form of a verb (Example: _Listen!_ or _Look out!_)
indefinite article	_a_ or _an_ used before a noun when something is talked about for the first time or when _the_ is too specific (Example: There's _a_ new _restaurant_ in town.)
infinitive	the main form of a verb, usually used with _to_ (Example: I like _to run_ fast.)
informal	friendly or casual language (Example: _Can_ I have that?)
irregular verb	a verb different from regular form verbs (Example: be = _am_, _are_, _is_, _was_, _were_, _being_)
modal auxiliary	a verb that indicates a mood (ability, possibility, etc.) and is followed by the base form of another verb (Example: I _can_ read English well.)

modifier	a word or phrase that describes another (Example: a _good_ friend)
negative	the opposite of affirmative (Example: She _does_ <u>not</u> _like_ meat.)
noun	a name of a person, place, or thing (Example: <u>_Joe_</u>, <u>_England_</u>, <u>_bottle_</u>)
noncount nouns	nouns impossible or difficult to count (Example: <u>_water_</u>, <u>_love_</u>, <u>_rice_</u>, <u>_fire_</u>)
object, direct	the noun or pronoun acted on by the verb (Example: I _eat_ <u>_oranges_</u>.)
object pronoun	replaces the noun taking the action (Example: _Julia_ is nice. I _like_ <u>_her_</u>.)
past tense	a verb form used to express an action or a state in the past (Example: You <u>_worked_</u> yesterday.)
period	a punctuation mark of a dot ending a sentence (.)
plural	indicating more than one (Example: _pencil<u>s</u>_, _child<u>ren</u>_)
possessive adjective	an adjective expressing possession (Example: <u>_our_</u> car)
preposition	a word that indicates relationship between objects (Example: <u>_on_</u> the _desk_)
present tense	a verb tense representing the current time, not past or future (Example: They <u>_are_</u> at home right now.)
pronoun	a word used in place of a noun (Example: _Ted_ is 65. <u>_He_</u> is retired.)
question form	to ask or look for an answer (Example: <u>_Where is my book?_</u>)
regular verb	verb with endings that are regular and follow the rule (Example: work = _work_, _work<u>s</u>_, _work<u>ed</u>_, _work<u>ing</u>_)
sentence	a thought expressed in words, with a subject and verb (Example: <u>_Julia works hard._</u>)
short answer	a response to a _yes/no_ question, usually a subject pronoun and auxiliary verb (Example: <u>_Yes, I am._</u> <u>_No, he doesn't._</u>)
singular	one object (Example: <u>_a cat_</u>)
statement	a sentence (Example: <u>_The weather is rainy today._</u>)
subject	the noun that does the action in a sentence (Example: <u>_The gardener_</u> works here.)
subject pronoun	a pronoun that takes the place of a subject (Example: _John_ is a student. <u>_He_</u> is smart.)
syllable	a part of a word as determined by vowel sounds and rhythm (Example: <u>_ta_</u>-<u>_ble_</u>)
tag questions	short informal questions that come at the end of a sentences in speech (Example: You like soup, <u>_don't you?_</u> They aren't hungry, <u>_are they?_</u>)
tense	the part of a verb that shows the past, present, or future time (Example: He _talk<u>ed</u>_.)
verb	word describing an action or state (Example: The boys <u>_walk_</u> to school; I <u>_am_</u> tired.)
vowels	the letters a, e, i, o, u, and sometimes y
_wh-_ questions	questions that ask for information, usually starting with _Who_, _What_, _When_, _Where_, or _Why_. (Example: <u>_Where_</u> do you live?) _How_ is often included in this group.
yes/no questions	questions that ask for an affirmative or a negative answer (Example: <u>_Are you_</u> <u>_happy?_</u>)

116   **Glossary of Grammar Terms**

➤ GRAMMAR REFERENCE

Simple Present: *Be*

Subject	Verb	Residence	Example sentence
I	am	from Mexico	I **am** from Mexico. (*I'm*)
we, you, they	are	single	We **are** single. (*We're*)
		23 years old	You **are** 23 years old. (*You're*)
he, she	is	divorced	He **is** divorced. (*He's*)
		from Vietnam	She **is** from Vietnam. (*She's*)

Negative Statements with *Be*

Subject	Negative *be*	Information	Contracted forms	
I	**am not**	nervous.	**I'm not**	—
You	**are not**	in Houston.	**you're not**	you **aren't**
He, She, It	**is not**	short.	he's, she's, it's not	he, she, it **isn't**
We	**are not**	hungry.	**we're not**	we **aren't**
They	**are not**	from Korea.	**they're not**	they **aren't**

- There is only one contracted form for *I am not: I'm not.*
- There are two contracted forms for the other negative forms of *be.*

Yes/No Questions with *Be*

Be	Subject	Information	Example question	Short answer
am	I	happy	**Am** I happy?	Yes, I am. / No, I'm not.
are	you	married	**Are** you married?	Yes, you are. / No, you're not.
	we	friends	**Are** we friends?	Yes, we are. / No, we're not.
	they	brothers	**Are** they brothers?	Yes, they are. / No, they're not.
is	he	from Italy	**Is** he from Italy?	Yes, he is. / No, he's not.
	she	in class today	**Is** she in class today?	Yes, she is. / No, she's not.
	it	sunny today	**Is** it sunny today?	Yes, it is. / No, it's not.

Questions with *Be*

Question word	Be	Singular or Plural
Where	is	the milk? the water? the oil?
Where	are	the eggs? the bananas? the pears?

Answers with *Be*

Subject	Be	Location
The milk / It	is	in Aisle 1.
The eggs / They	are	in Aisle 5.

Simple Present

Subject	Verb	Information	Example sentence
I, you, we, they	eat	lunch	I always **eat** lunch at 4:00 P.M.
	go	to school	You often **go** to school at 8:00 A.M.
	help	with the children	We sometimes **help** with the children.
	play	soccer	They never **play** soccer on Saturday.
he, she	eats	lunch	He rarely **eats** lunch at 12:00 P.M.
	goes	to school	Nadia always **goes** to school early.
	helps	with the children	Gilberto never **helps** with the children.
	plays	soccer	She sometimes **plays** soccer on Friday.

Affirmative Simple Present

I	wear	
you	like	
we	want	
they	need	shoes
he	wears	
	likes	
she	wants	
	needs	

Negative Simple Present

I		wear	
you	do not	like	
we	(don't)		sandals
they		want	
he	does not	need	
she	(doesn't)		

Simple Present: *Yes/No Questions*

Yes/No question			Short answer	
Do	I you we they	**need** a coat?	Yes, you **do**. Yes, I **do**. Yes, we **do**. Yes, they **do**.	No, you **don't**. No, I **don't**. No, we **don't**. No, they **don't**.
Does	he she it	**wear** sweaters?	Yes, he **does**. Yes, she **does**. Yes, it **does**.	No, he **doesn't**. No, she **doesn't**. No, it **doesn't**.

- Use *do* with *I, you, we, they*, and plural subjects.
- Use *does* with *he, she, it*, and singular subjects.
- Always use the base form after *do* or *does*.

Simple Present: *Live*

Subject	Verb	Residence	Example sentence
I, we, you, they	live	in Los Angeles in California	I **live** in Los Angeles. You **live** in Los Angeles, California.
he, she	lives	in the United States in Mexico	He **lives** in the United States. She **lives** in Mexico.

Simple Present: *Have*

Subject	Have	Information	Example sentence
I, you, we, they	have	three brothers two sisters	I **have** three brothers. We **have** two sisters.
he, she	has	no cousins three sons	He **has** no cousins. She **has** three sons.

Negative: *Have*

Subject	Negative	Have	Information	Example Sentence
I, you, we, they	don't	have	three brothers two sisters	I **don't have** three brothers. We **don't have** three sisters.
he, she	doesn't		cousins three sons	He **doesn't have** cousins. She **doesn't have** three sons.

Yes/No Questions: *Is it?*

Question + verb	Information	Question	Answer Yes	Answer No
Is it	hot windy cloudy rainy snowy cold foggy	**Is it** hot outside? **Is it** windy today? **Is it** cloudy in Florida? **Is it** rainy there? **Is it** snowy in the mountains? **Is it** cold in Chicago? **Is it** foggy in the morning?	Yes, **it is.**	No, **it isn't.**

Information Questions with *Be* and *Do*

Information word	Be	Information	Example answer
How much (money)	is	the rent?	$1,500 a month.
	are	the flowers?	$20.00.
Where	is	the apartment?	On First Street.
	are	the apartments?	
What kind of home	is	for rent?	An apartment.
What kinds of homes	are	in the neighborhood?	Apartments and houses.

Information word	Do + subject	Base verb	Example answer
How much (money)	do you	have?	$20.00.
Where	do you	live?	On First Street.
What kind of home	do you	have?	An apartment.
What kinds of homes	do you		Apartments and houses.
How many bedrooms	does it	have?	Three.

Information Question	Example answer
What is your name?	My name is Javier Aguilar.
Where do you live now?	I live in Santa Clara.
Where did you live before?	I lived in Richmond.
How long did you live there?	I lived there three years.
Who is your employer?	I work for Anchor Motors.
What is your position?	I am a mechanic.

Information Questions with *which*

Information word	Subject	Verb	Information	Example question
which	house	has	three bedrooms	Which house has three bedrooms?
	houses	have	a pool / a fireplace / a big yard	Which houses have three bedrooms?
	house	is	on First Street / next to the park	Which house is on First Street?
	houses	are		Which houses are on First Street? / Which houses are next to the park?

Present Continuous

Subject	Be	Base+*ing*	Example sentence
I	am	writing	I **am writing** this letter in English.
you, we, they	are	going	We **are going** to the mall.
he, she	is	eating	He **is eating** at the coffee shop.

- Use simple present with *always, often, usually, never, sometimes,* and *every day.*
- Use the present continuous with *right now, at this moment,* and *today.*

Affirmative Present Continuous

Subject	Be	Base + *ing*	
I	am	wearing	right now
you, we, they	are	buying going	at this moment
he, she, it	is	shopping eating	today

Negative Present Continuous

Subject	Be	*not*	Base + *ing*	
I (I'm)	am	not	waiting buying	right now
you, we, they	are	not (aren't)	going	at this moment
he, she, it	is	not (isn't)	shopping eating	today

Present Continuous: *Yes/No Questions*

Be	Subject	Base verb + *ing*	Short answer	
Am	I	**going** with you to the mall?	Yes, you **are.**	No, you **aren't.**
Are	you	**shopping** today?	Yes, I **am.**	No, I'm **not.**
Is	he, she, it	**wearing** a sweater?	Yes, he/she/it **is.**	No, he/she/it **isn't.**
Are	we	**buying** new jeans now?	Yes, we **are.**	No, we **aren't.**
Are	they	**having** a sale right now?	Yes, they **are.**	No, they **aren't.**

Regular Simple Past	
Subject	**Verb (base + *ed*)**
I, you, he, she, we, they	walked (walk) talked (talk) smoked (smoke) played (play)

Irregular Simple Past	
Subject	**Verb**
I, you, he, she, we, they	had (have) went (go) said (say)

Irregular Simple Past: *Be*		
Subject	**Be verb**	**Example sentence**
I, he, she	was	I **was** sick.
you, we, they	were	You **were** at the hospital.

Simple Past (Regular)		
Subject	**Verb (base+*ed*)**	**Example sentence**
I, you, he, she, it, we, they	talked wanted walked	I **talked** with Marie. She **wanted** a sandwich. We **walked** in the park.

Simple Past (Irregular)		
Subject	**Verb**	**Example sentence**
I, you, he, she, it, we, they	went (go) ate (eat) bought (buy) sent (send)	I **went** to the park. She **ate** at the coffee shop. We **bought** new dresses. They **sent** a letter.

Simple Past: Questions	
Yes/No Question	**Short answer**
Did you **exercise** yesterday?	Yes, I **did**. No, I **didn't**.
Did he **have** an earache?	Yes, he **did**. No, he **didn't**.
Did we **buy** any aspirin?	Yes, we **did**. No, we **didn't**.

- For *yes/no* questions in the simple past tense (regular or irregular verbs), use *did* + the base form.

Information Question	Answer
Where **did** you **play** soccer yesterday?	I played soccer in the park.
How **did** she **get** to the doctor's office?	She took the bus.
When **did** they **have** an appointment?	They had an appointment at 3:00.

- For information questions in the simple past tense, use *did* + the base form.

Simple Past

Negative forms of regular and irregular verbs (except *be*)	
I **didn't work** in the evenings.	We **didn't have** a paid vacation.
Dalva **didn't know** how to type.	You **didn't turn off** the computer.

- For all forms of regular and irregular verbs (except *be*), use *did not* (*didn't*) + base.

Negative forms of *be*	
I **wasn't** at work today. He/She/It **wasn't** friendly.	We **weren't** happy. You **weren't** in the hospital. They **weren't** at the front desk.

- For the verb *be*, use *was not* (*wasn't*) and *were not* (*weren't*).

Questions with *Can*

Can	Subject	Base verb	Example sentence
can	I	take help	Can I take your order? Can I help you?
can	you		Can you take my order? Can you take our order, please? Can you help me? Can you help us?

Questions with *May* and *Can*

Can	Subject	Base verb	Example question and answer
can	I, you, he, she, it, we, they	type	Can you type letters? Yes, I can.
		drive	Can they drive a car? No, they can't.
		understand	Can she understand English? Yes, she can.
		work	Can I work on Saturdays? Yes, you can.
		cook	Can he cook breakfast? No, he can't.
		clean	Can we clean on the weekend? Yes, you can.
		talk	Can you talk to customers? No, you can't.

Modal: *Can* (Ability)

	Subject	*Can*	Base verb	Example sentence
Affirmative	I	**can**	type	I **can** type 60 words a minute.
	he, she, it	**can**	use	He/ She **can** use a computer.
	we	**can**	fix	We **can** fix things around the house.
Negative	you	**cannot**	speak	You **cannot** speak Spanish.
	they	**can't**	turn	They **can't** turn on the copier.

- The negative of *can* is *cannot*. The contraction is *can't*.

Modals: *May* and *Might* to Show Probability (Use Interchangeably)

Subject	Modal	Base verb	Example sentence
I, you, he, she, it, we, they	may might	spend earn be	I **may** spend $250 on gasoline this month. You **may** spend $175 on the phone bill. He **may** earn $6,000. Food **might** be $1,000. We **may** earn $3,500 a month. They **may** spend $300 a month on food.

Questions with *Should*

Yes/No Question	Short answer
Should I **exercise** every day?	Yes, you **should**. No, you **shouldn't**.
Should he **have** a checkup?	Yes, he **should**. No, he **shouldn't**.
Should we **buy** some vitamins?	Yes, we **should**. No, we **shouldn't**.
Information Question	**Answer**
Who **should** I **ask** about the medicine?	You **should** ask the doctor.
Where **should** she **buy** the cough syrup?	She **should** buy the cough syrup at the pharmacy.
Why **should** we **take** the pills?	We have a cough and a fever.

- For *Yes/No* questions and information questions, use *should* + the base form.

Modal: *Should*

Subject	*Should*	Base verb	Example sentence
I, you, he, she, we, they	should	take talk take swallow	I **should** take two tablets. He **should** talk to the doctor. You **should** take this medicine for a headache. They **should** swallow this tablet with water.

Modal: *Shouldn't*

Subject	*Should*	Base verb	Example sentence
I, you, he, she, we, they	should not shouldn't	take chew drink	You **shouldn't** take this pill with other medicine. He **shouldn't** drink alcohol with this medicine. She **shouldn't** chew this tablet.

Future: *Will*

Subject	*Will*	Base verb	Information
I, you, he, she, it, we, they	will	go study be	to school for two more years English this year a nurse

want to	*hope to*	*plan to*	*be going to*	*will*

less definite ——————————————————————→ very definite

Future: *Will* (Affirmative)

Subject	*Will*	Base verb	Example sentence
I, you, he, she, we, they	will	come listen help work have	I **will** come to class on time. You **will** listen carefully and follow instructions. They **will** help other students. We **will** work hard. He **will** have a positive attitude.

Future: *Will* (Negative)

Subject	*Will*	Base verb	Example sentence
I, you, he, she, we, they	will not (won't)	come leave forget	I **won't** come to class late. I **won't** leave class early. I **won't** forget my homework.

Yes/No Questions with *Will*

Statement	Question	Answer	
I will be rich some day.	**Will** I **be** rich some day?	Yes, you will.	No, you won't.
You will start college next year.	**Will** you **start** college next year?	Yes, I will.	No, I won't.
He will find a job.	**Will** he **find** a job?	Yes, he will.	No, he won't.
She will get some advice.	**Will** she **get** some advice?	Yes, she will.	No, she won't.
It will be closed.	**Will** it **be** closed?	Yes, it will.	No, it won't.
We will work together.	**Will** we **work** together?	Yes, we will.	No, we won't.
They will handle the money.	**Will** they **handle** the money?	Yes, they will.	No, they won't.

Express Future Plans: *want to, hope to, plan to*

Subject	Verb	Infinitive (*to* + base)	
I, you, we, they	hope, want, plan	to	study in school for three years graduate from college get married be a doctor
he, she	hopes, wants, plans		

Express Future Plans: *Be going to*

Subject	*Be going to*	Base verb	Information
I	am going to	get	a high school diploma
you, we, they	are going to	participate	in my child's school
he, she	is going to	buy	a house

| Will/Be going to: Information Questions ||
Wh- word + will + subject + base verb	Wh- word + be + subject + going to + base verb
What **will** you do tomorrow?	What **are** you **going to** do tomorrow?
What time **will** she leave?	What time **is** she **going to** leave?
How **will** you pay for school?	How **are** you **going to** pay for school?
When **will** they arrive?	When **are** they **going to** arrive?
How much time **will** the students have?	How much time **are** the students **going to** have?
How long **will** they stay?	How long **are** they **going to** stay?
How often **will** you take a trip?	How often **are** you **going to** take a trip?
Where **will** she live?	Where **is** she **going to** live?

| Using *Because* ||||
Statement	*Because*	Reason Subject + verb	Example sentence
I want the blue shirt	because	it is cheaper	I want the blue shirt **because** it is cheaper.
I shop at Addy's	because	it is close	I shop at Addy's **because** it is close to my home.
You like the shirt	because	it is green	You like the shirt **because** it is green.

| *Because* and Adverbial Clauses ||||
Statement		Reason Subject + verb	Information
Maria plans to go to college	because	she wants	to be a nurse
Lien hopes to learn English better	because	she plans	to go to college

Examples: Maria plans to go to college **because** she wants to be a nurse.

Lien hopes to learn English **because** she plans to go to college.

Usage:
- Usually you do not write a comma after or before *because*.
- A subject always follows *because*.

Combining Sentences with *and*

Subject		Subject	
The house	<u>is</u> in a quiet neighborhood.	The house	<u>has</u> a swimming pool.
The house	<u>is</u> in a quiet neighborhood, **and** **it**		<u>has</u> a swimming pool.
The house is in a quiet neighborhood, **and it** has a swimming pool.			

Combining Sentences with *and*

Subject		Subject	
The rooms	<u>have</u> air-conditioning.	The rooms	<u>are</u> in good condition.
The rooms	<u>have</u> air-conditioning, **and** **they**		<u>are</u> in good condition.
The rooms have air-conditioning, **and they** are in good condition.			

Verb + Infinitive

Subject	Verb	Infinitive (*to* + base)		Example sentence
I, you, we, they	want	to	sleep	I **want to sleep** eight hours.
	need		relax	You **need to relax** after work.
	like		work	We **like to work** in the morning.
he, she	wants		drink	They **want to drink** a lot of water.
	needs		eat	He **likes to eat** a snack in the afternoon.
	likes		exercise	She **likes to exercise** regularly.

Imperatives

Affirmative imperative	Negative imperative
Write your name on the application.	**Don't write** your age.
Press the green button.	**Don't press** the red button.
Be helpful at work.	**Don't be** late for work.

- The imperative uses the base form of the verb.
- The subject is **you**, but it is not included.
- The negative imperative is *do not* + base form. The contraction is *don't*.
- Imperatives give warnings, directions, or suggestions.
- Use an exclamation mark (!) if the feeling is very strong.

Adjective	Comparative adjective	Example sentence
cheap	cheaper	The shirt is **cheaper** *than* the dress.
expensive	more expensive	The shoes are **more expensive** *than* the shirt.
	less expensive	The dress is **less expensive** *than* the jacket.

Adjective	Superlatives	Example sentence
cheap	cheapest	The socks are the **cheapest**.
expensive	most expensive	The jacket is the **most expensive**.
	least expensive	The socks are the **least expensive**.

Adjectives and noun modifiers	
Adjectives	**Noun modifiers**
Adjectives describe nouns. I live in a **friendly** neighborhood.	A noun can sometimes describe another noun. I need a **coffee** table.
Adjectives come before nouns. He likes the **big** yard.	The second noun is more general than the first. A **coffee** table is usually small.
Adjectives do not change for plural nouns. You're buying some **new** tables.	The first noun is always singular. Where are the **coffee** tables?
You can put two adjectives before a noun. Use a comma between the adjectives. We want a **large, old** house.	You can put a number before a noun modifier. Use a hyphen between the number and the modifier. You want a **two-bedroom** apartment. (Meaning: two bedrooms, not two apartments)

Transition Words in Sentences		
With numbers	**Without numbers**	**Example sentence**
First (First of all)	First	**First of all**, I went to town. **First**, I went to town.
Second	Next	**Second**, I ate. / **Next**, I ate.
Third	Then	**Third**, I saw a movie. / **Then**, I saw a movie.
	After that	**After that**, I had a soda.
Finally / Lastly	Finally	**Lastly**, I went home. / **Finally**, I went home.

- Do not use numbers as transition words if there are more than four steps.
- When not using numbers, *next, then*, and *after that* can be used in any order to describe more than one step.
- Always finish with the words *finally* or *lastly*.

Possessive Adjectives

Pronoun	Possessive adjective	Example sentence
I	my	**My** address is 3356 Archer Blvd.
you	your	**Your** phone number is 555-5678.
he	his	**His** last name is Jones.
she	her	**Her** first name is Lien.
it	its	**Its** name is Crystal River Dam.
we	our	**Our** teacher is Mr. Kelley.
they	their	**Their** home is in Sausalito.

Demonstrative Adjectives: *this, that, these, those*

	Near	Far
Singular	this sweater this hat	that sweater that hat
Plural	these shoes these pants	those shoes those pants

Example sentences		
	Near	Far
Singular	**This** sweater is perfect. I want **this** hat.	**That** sweater is blue. I like **that** hat.
Plural	**These** pants fit. I like **these** shoes.	**Those** pants are great! I like **those** shoes.

How much / How many

Count nouns	Noncount nouns
Use *many* with nouns you can count.	Use *much* with nouns you cannot count.

Example Questions	
How many tomatoes do we need?	**How much** flour do we need?
How many pounds of tomatoes do we need?	**How much** rice do we need?

There is / There are	
Singular	There is (There's) a good Vietnamese restaurant in Portland.
	There is (There's) one bottle of soda for lunch.
Plural	There are carrots in Aisle 4.
	There are three pieces of cake.
Questions	Is there a dairy section in this supermarket?
	Are there many Chinese restaurants in Los Angeles?

- Use *there* to show or ask about place or position.

Some / Any		
	Count (Plural)	**Noncount**
Affirmative	I eat **some** vegetables every day.	I often eat **some** rice for dinner.
Negative	I don't eat **any** cookies.	I don't eat **any** rice.
Question	Do you have **any** cookies?	Do you have **any** rice?
	Do you want **some** cookies?	Do you want **some** rice?

- In questions that are requests or offers, use *some*.

Prepositions of Location	
Preposition	**Example**
in	There is a hospital **in** Thomasville.
on	It is **on** Main Street.
at	It is **at** the intersection of Main Street and Northern Avenue.
near	It is **near** my house.
between	My house is **between** South Street and Washington Street.
next to	It is **next to** the police station.
on the corner (of)	The police station is **on the corner of** South Street and Pine Street.
across from	It is **across from** the post office.
on the right	The courthouse is **on the right**.
on the left	The fire station is **on the left**.

Prepositions of Time		
Preposition	**Information**	**Example sentence**
on	days	I am going to the bank **on** Saturday.
	dates	City Hall is not open **on** July 4.
at	a specific time	I am going to the dentist **at** 3:00 P.M.
	night	We go to the library **at** night.
in	amount of time	He's going to Japan **in** two hours.
	months	He always visits his sister **in** August.
	seasons	The weather is very warm **in** the summer.
	the morning / afternoon / evening	We go to the bowling alley **in** the afternoon.

Grammar Reference

➤ IRREGULAR SIMPLE PAST VERB LIST

Base form	Simple past form	Base form	Simple past form
be	was, were	make	made
break	broke	pay	paid
buy	bought	put	put
can	could	read	read
choose	chose	run	ran
come	came	say	said
cut	cut	see	saw
do	did	sell	sold
draw	drew	send	sent
drink	drank	shut	shut
drive	drove	sit	sat
eat	ate	sleep	slept
find	found	speak	spoke
get	got	spend	spent
go	went	swim	swam
give	gave	take	took
have	had	teach	taught
hear	heard	understand	understood
hurt	hurt	wake	woke
keep	kept	wear	wore
know	knew	write	wrote

➤ CONJUGATED VERB LIST

Regular verbs

Base: work   **Infinitive:** to work

Simple present	Present continuous	Simple past	Future
I work	I am working	I worked	I will work
you work	you are working	you worked	you will work
we work	we are working	we worked	we will work
they work	they are working	they worked	they will work
he works	he is working	he worked	he will work
she works	she is working	she worked	she will work
it works	it is working	it worked	it will work

Base: live   **Infinitive:** to live

Simple present	Present continuous	Simple past	Future
I live	I am living	I lived	I will live
you live	you are living	you lived	you will live
we live	we are living	we lived	we will live
they live	they are living	they lived	they will live
he lives	he is living	he lived	he will live
she lives	she is living	she lived	she will live
it lives	it is living	it lived	it will live

Base: study   **Infinitive:** to study

Simple present	Present continuous	Simple past	Future
I study	I am studying	I studied	I will study
you study	you are studying	you studied	you will study
we study	we are studying	we studied	we will study
they study	they are studying	they studied	they will study
he studies	he is studying	he studied	he will study
she studies	she is studying	she studied	she will study
it studies	it is studying	it studied	it will study

Base: stop   **Infinitive:** to stop

Simple present	Present continuous	Simple past	Future
I stop	I am stopping	I stopped	I will stop
you stop	you are stopping	you stopped	you will stop
we stop	we are stopping	we stopped	we will stop
they stop	they are stopping	they stopped	they will stop
he stops	he is stopping	he stopped	he will stop
she stops	she is stopping	she stopped	she will stop
it stops	it is stopping	it stopped	it will stop

Irregular verbs

Base: be   **Infinitive:** to be

Simple present	Present continuous	Simple past	Future
I am	I am being	I was	I will be
you are	you are being	you were	you will be
we are	we are being	we were	we will be
they are	they are being	they were	they will be
he is	he is being	he was	he will be
she is	she is being	she was	she will be
it is	it is being	it was	it will be

Base: have   **Infinitive:** to have

Simple present	Present continuous	Simple past	Future
I have	I am having	I had	I will have
you have	you are having	you had	you will have
we have	we are having	we had	we will have
they have	they are having	they had	they will have
he has	he is having	he had	he will have
she has	she is having	she had	she will have
it has	it is having	it had	it will have

Base: go   **Infinitive:** to go

Simple present	Present continuous	Simple past	Future
I go	I am going	I went	I will go
you go	you are going	you went	you will go
we go	we are going	we went	we will go
they go	they are going	they went	they will go
he goes	he is going	he went	he will go
she goes	she is going	she went	she will go
it goes	it is going	it went	it will go

Base: run   **Infinitive:** to run

Simple present	Present continuous	Simple past	Future
I run	I am running	I ran	I will run
you run	you are running	you ran	you will run
we run	we are running	we ran	we will run
they run	they are running	they ran	they will run
he runs	he is running	he ran	he will run
she runs	she is running	she ran	she will run
it runs	it is running	it ran	it will run

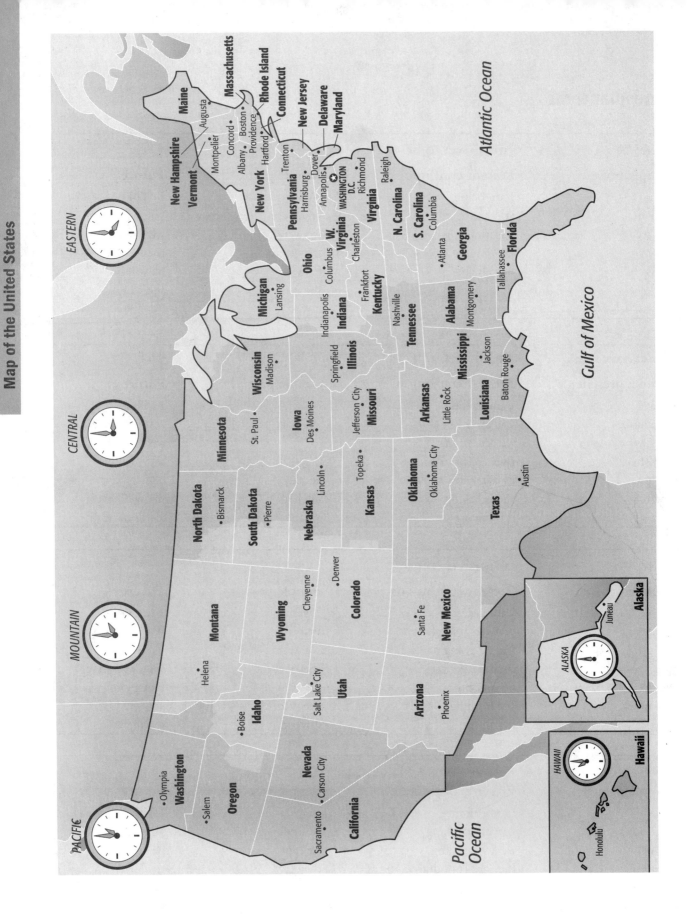

Map of the United States